The Canadian Multinationals

Date Due

I.A. Litvak and C.J. Maule

BUTTERWORTHS
Toronto

The Canadian Multinationals
©1981 Butterworth & Co. (Canada) Ltd.

Printed and bound in Canada

The Butterworth Group of Companies

Canada:
Butterworth & Co. (Canada) Ltd., Toronto
Butterworth & Co. (Western Canada) Ltd., Vancouver

United Kingdom:
Butterworth & Co. (Publishers) Ltd., London, Borough Green

Australia:
Butterworths Pty. Ltd., Sydney, Melbourne, Brisbane, Perth, Norwood

New Zealand:
Butterworths of New Zealand Ltd., Wellington

South Africa:
Butterworth & Co. (South Africa) Ltd., Durban

United States:
Butterworth (Publishers) Inc., Boston
Butterworth (Legal Publishers) Inc., Seattle
Butterworth & Co. Ltd., Ann Arbor
Mason Publishing Company, St. Paul

Canadian Cataloguing in Publication Data

Litvak, I. A. (Isaiah A.), 1936-
   The Canadian multinationals

ISBN 0-409-84525-6

1. Investments, Canadian. 2. Corporations, Canadian.
3. International business enterprises.
I. Maule, C. J. (Christopher J.), 1934-
II. Title.

HG5152.L57   332.6'7371   C81-094076-0

Printed by Alger Press Ltd.
Cover design by Julian Cleva

31591
JUN 1 1981

HG
5152
L57

Preface

A few years ago it became clear that the interest and concern which had been given to foreign investment in Canada was not in evidence for Canadian investment abroad. From time to time certain incidents would receive publicity, such as the nationalization of Alcan's bauxite operations in Guyana, layoffs by Inco in Sudbury at a time when the company was investing in Guatemala and Indonesia, Canadian investment in South Africa, and Northern Telecom's expansion by way of manufacturing and research and development in the U.S. However, there has been no body of research findings which examines the extent and nature of Canadian direct investment abroad, its impact on Canada and the policy alternatives which need to be considered.

In order to fill this research gap, the authors initiated a series of individual research projects which would throw light on some of these issues. The findings were published in the *Business Quarterly*, the *International Journal*, and the *Journal of World Trade Law*.[1] Some of the material contained in Chapters 1 to 5 has been drawn from these journal articles.[2] The material in Chapter 6 deals with a new topic, Codes of Conduct, which is relevant both to inward and outward investment. Codes of Conduct is a policy approach, which is receiving considerable attention in the international forum as well as in individual countries.

This book is not a systematic treatment of all economic and political aspects of Canadian investment abroad. It does, however, deal with a number of important topics, namely the extent and nature of Canadian investment abroad, the major corporate investors, reasons why small and medium-sized firms invest in the U.S., the economic impact of outward investment on Canada, the existing Canadian policies and the relevance of Codes of Conduct.

The authors would like to acknowledge the financial assistance received over the years in connection with this research from the Donner Canadian Foundation, the Canada Council, the Department of Industry, Trade and Commerce, the Norman Paterson School of International Affairs at Carleton University, and the Faculty of Administrative Studies at York University. We are also indebted to Barry Boothman for his invaluable research assistance, to Norma Rankin for the efficient way in which the manuscript was typed and prepared for publication, and to Jody O'Brien for her editorial work.

In the text that follows please note that all dollar figures are in Canadian funds unless otherwise noted.

NOTES

1. "Canadian Multinationals in the Western Hemisphere", *The Business Quarterly*, Vol. 40, No. 3, (Autumn 1975), pp. 30-42; "The Emerging Challenge of Canadian Direct Investment Abroad", *The Business Quarterly*, Vol. 43, No. 1, (Spring 1978), pp. 24-37; "Canadian Small Business Investment in the U.S. — Corporate Forms and Characteristics", *The Business Quarterly*, (Winter 1978), Vol. 43, No. 4, pp. 69-79; "Canadian Investment Abroad: In Search of a Policy", *International Journal*, Vol. 31, No. 1, (Winter 1975-76), pp. 159-179; and "Canadian Outward Investment — Impact and Policy", *Journal of World Trade Law*, Vol. 14, No. 4, (July-August 1980), pp. 310-328.
2. The authors would like to acknowledge the kind permission of the Journals to use these previously published materials.

Contents

Chapter 1

Introduction

Canadian direct investment abroad increased 4½ times between 1960 and 1978 through the establishment of new facilities, the takeover of foreign firms, and involvement in joint ventures. Much of this investment has been financed through borrowing in foreign financial markets, and through investing the retained earnings of existing foreign affiliates abroad. Some of the reasons offered by Canadian businessmen for investing abroad include domestic market saturation, the desire for growth, gaining access to foreign markets, scarcity of certain factors of production in Canada, the need to gain access to raw materials abroad, and tax and other financial advantages acquired when investing abroad. From time to time, the general economic and political climate in Canada has spurred firms to invest abroad.

In the 1960s, the corporate motivation for investing abroad was viewed largely in positive terms. Firms felt that growth was necessary in order to compete internationally, and that the limitations imposed by the small Canadian market needed to be broken. The bulk of this investment was undertaken by resource based firms in Canada, as a means of diversifying their operations both in geographic and product terms. Motivation for investing abroad in the late 1970s has been greatly accelerated by negative considerations as well, such as Canada's high inflation rates, government controls on prices, profits, and executive salaries, strikes, union militancy, poor labour/management relations, federal/provincial jurisdictional disputes over natural resources, provincial expropriation of foreign firms, and the general political and economic uncertainties surrounding Quebec's aspirations for independence.

Direct investment abroad by Canadian companies is emerging as a major topic for debate in Canada. The concern expressed is twofold. First, such investment by Canadian businessmen is viewed as a vote of non-confidence in the state and future of Canada's economy. Press announcements of Canadian firms acquiring or establishing new commercial operations abroad, particularly in the United States, have received regular attention in daily newspapers. The firms identified include both giant corporations such as Inco, which acquired ESB, a major battery manufacturer in the United States, as well as small firms like a Montreal photo products manufacturer which opened a $300,000 plant

1

in New York State. Second, attention is drawn to the potential negative impact of such investment on Canada's economy. For example, expanding abroad can be an alternative to expanding at home. By producing abroad to service local markets, unions and politicians have argued that domestic employment is being exported. Moreover, it is contended that such investment will result in a significant drop in Canadian exports, and thereby result in further deterioration of Canada's balance of payments. Both consequences were highlighted in the context of Inco's 1977 announcement to cut back nickel production and employment in Canada, while bringing on stream its new nickel deposits in Indonesia and Guatemala.

This negative view of the impact of such investment on the capital exporting country is not unique to Canada. A similar debate occurred in the United States with much greater intensity in the early 1970s. In response to such charges, raised especially by unions, the U.S. government launched a major study to examine the impact and effects of direct investment abroad. The findings refuted most of the charges, claiming that such investment was indeed beneficial to the U.S. economy.[1]

Canadian controlled firms are recent entrants to the field of multinational business compared to their European, Japanese and U.S. counterparts. Nonetheless, their numbers are growing, particularly with reference to their investments in the western hemisphere. However, as these firms expand their investment activities in the United States, which is usually a forerunner to expansion into Latin America, their investment and the U.S. market tend to dominate much of the attention of Canadian corporate management. Increasing pre-occupation with the U.S. subsidiary often overshadows the time devoted to the Canadian market, which is the base operation of the parent company. This phenomenon has profound implications for the companies' global strategy and structure, and their view of themselves as Canadian companies.

The fact that the U.S. government and its business community are becoming more chauvinistic and protectionist towards foreign multinationals will in all likelihood accelerate the Americanization of Canadian multinationals, rather differently from the U.S. impact on European and Japanese multinationals. The impact could affect both the U.S. subsidiary and the Canadian parent so that key parts of the Canadian corporate infrastructure will become situated in the U.S., servicing not only the U.S. subsidiary, but also its Canadian parent and *their* overseas operations. This phenomenon is already taking hold in some Canadian multinationals, partly assisted by the increasing U.S. share ownership of these enterprises, which are also listed on the U.S. stock exchange.

There are a number of domestic and foreign policy reasons why Canada should be concerned about investment abroad. First, Canada's principal trading partner and foreign investor in Canada, the U.S., is also the recipient of over half of Canada's investment abroad. The consequences of outward investment as well as trade and inward investment, need to be considered in economic negotiations with the U.S. Second, policy positions have been taken in a vacuum to date, because it is not known what the economic and political impacts of outward investment are on Canada. No detailed study has been undertaken. For example, it can be argued that the export performance of Canadian firms is a mixture of their ability to export from Canada, plus their ability to service foreign markets from the sales of subsidiaries in those markets.

Third, there are a number of government policies which affect Canadian direct investment abroad (CDIA), but there has been no attempt to ensure the consistency of these policies. Canada does have detailed policies with respect to inward investment. In dealings with other countries, its position on outward investment should be consistent with its position on inward investment.

Fourth, a peculiarity of the Canadian situation is that a significant part of CDIA is undertaken by foreign owned, mainly U.S., enterprises. In representations to foreign governments on behalf of Canadian based corporations, the Canadian government may find itself acting on behalf of foreign owned corporations.

Fifth, the issue of foreign investment, inward and outward, is of increasing importance to Canada's international relations. It is present in the contractual link with the European Economic Community, in other commercial agreements, in assistance to developing countries, in government sponsored cartel agreements, as in the case of uranium and potash, and in dealings with countries such as South Africa and Chile.

Finally, it is possible that investment wars could develop between capital exporting and host countries as policies are introduced which attempt to tilt production and employment towards their economies.[2] These wars could be comparable to the trade wars of the 1930s and would be detrimental to both national and global welfare. Canada is a combatant when it offers financial assistance to U.S. automobile companies.

The remaining chapters of the book deal with a number of these issues. In Chapter 2, an examination is made of the extent and nature of Canada's outward investment, focusing on the aggregate statistics and the principal investing firms. Outward investment is concentrated in relatively few firms, and the U.S. is the market where most of the investment is located. Overall, more than 75% of the investment is in the developed countries and has been for some time. At the other end of the corporate spectrum, there are a number of small and medium-sized Canadian firms which invest abroad. The reasons a group of these firms have invested in the U.S. market in recent years is the subject of Chapter 3. The companies studied stressed the view that their move into the U.S. market was made in order to sustain their competitiveness in Canada.

That is to say, they felt that success in the larger U.S. market would ensure their success in Canada. Undoubtedly, the deteriorating economic and political conditions in Canada at the time this study was made reinforced their decision to expand into the U.S. market, but these conditions alone would not have prompted the move.

The impact of outward investment on Canada in the case of Alcan, Inco and Northern Telecom is analyzed in Chapter 4. Here it is shown that the nature of the impact depends crucially on the assumptions made about the conditions which would have existed in the absence of the outward investment. For these three companies, it is argued that the impact on Canada in terms of employment and balance of payments has generally been favourable. This finding is similar to that resulting from case studies made of the impact on the U.S. of outward investment.

Canada does have a sprinkling of ill-coordinated policies on outward investment. These are examined in Chapter 5, especially the cases of the Export Development Corporation and the Canadian International Development Agency. The Canadian government's hesitant support for Alcan when its operations in Guyana were nationalized is also documented in this chapter.

Finally, Chapter 6 examines the development and use of guidelines and Codes of Conduct for the behaviour of foreign subsidiaries. These Codes have been developed for a number of purposes, but in recent years, two issues have received particular attention: first, *Questionable and Illegal Corporate Payments,* and second, the case of foreign investment in South Africa. There is some possibility that the OECD guidelines for foreign investment, which have been accepted by certain developed countries, may also be acceptable to the less developed countries. Even though guidelines and codes are not enforceable, they may go part way towards removing some of the irritants associated with foreign investment.

In sum, our research has led us to the conclusion that Canada has about $14 billion worth of outward investment compared to five times as much inward investment. However, relative to the size of the Canadian economy, the outward investment is not an inconsequential amount. Second, small and medium-sized firms tend to be attracted to investing in the U.S. market because of the size and proximity of that market. Third, the impact of outward investment on Canada, in terms of the several cases examined in some depth, appears to be beneficial to Canada. Fourth, Canadian policy on outward investment does exist, but is in a rudimentary state and is ill-coordinated. Finally, recent attempts to develop guidelines and codes of conduct, even though they are not enforceable, may have some chance of acceptance by developed and developing nations and thereby have some hope of alleviating friction between host and home countries.

The Canadian government will continue to respond in an ad hoc and inconsistent manner to issues arising from outward investment, unless an attempt is made to analyze and understand the issues. Failure to do so may lead more Canadian companies to gravitate towards the larger U.S. market, and once there, to treat the Canadian operations as a subsidiary of lesser importance. If the parent companies do migrate to the U.S., then head offices will move together with functional activities such as research and development. The number of lost jobs may not be great, but these will be jobs requiring high level skills. Once this migration starts, and it has already taken place from Montreal to other Canadian cities, there will be a demonstration effect for companies of all sizes. At best, the examination of outward investment deserves a reasonable fraction of the attention which has been lavished on the subject of inward investment in Canada over the past 25 years.

NOTES

1. This and other studies are reviewed in Chapter 4.
2. C. F. Bergsten, "Coming Investment Wars?", in *Foreign Affairs*, Vol. 53, (October, 1974), p. 135.

Chapter 2

Profiles of Canadian Multinationals

NATURE AND EXTENT OF CANADIAN DIRECT INVESTMENT ABROAD

Canadian direct investment abroad runs at about one-fifth of direct investment in Canada. Since much of this inward investment is U.S. controlled, Canadian attention has been focussed largely on the behaviour and operations of U.S. multinational enterprises. Canada, however, is not without its multinational representatives. Their numbers and size have been increasing in recent years. Canadian direct investment abroad (CDIA) quintupled from $2.5 billion in 1960 to $11.5 billion in 1976, and to at least $14 billion by 1978.[1] By the end of 1976, the United States accounted for approximately 53% of total CDIA, the United Kingdom 9%, the European Economic Community (excluding the U.K.) 6%, other European countries 2%, Australasia 5%, and Japan 0.6% (see Table 1). As a group, these countries accounted for approximately 76% of CDIA. The industrial distribution of CDIA in 1976 was approximately 50% in manufacturing, with more than half of it centred in the United States; 23% in mining and petroleum; 14% in utilities; 4% in merchandising; and 11% in other industrial categories (see Table 2).

Table 1

CANADIAN DIRECT INVESTMENT ABROAD BY LOCATION OF INVESTMENT IN 1976

Location	Year Ended 1976 ($millions)	% of Total	Location	Year Ended 1976 ($millions)	% of Total
NORTH AMERICA & CARIBBEAN:					
United States	6,052	52.81	Jamaica	102	
Mexico	68		Trinidad & Tabago	24	
Bahamas	135		Other	128	
Bermuda	439		Sub-Total	6,948	60.63

6

Location	Year Ended 1976 ($millions)	% of Total	Location	Year Ended 1976 ($millions)	% of Total
SOUTH & CENTRAL AMERICA:			NON-EEC COUNTRIES:		
			Switzerland	107	
Venezuela	25		Norway	60	
Argentina	46		Spain	53	
Brazil	1,157		Other	70	
Other	142		Sub-Total	290	2.53
Sub-Total	1,370	11.95	Sub-Total	2,033	17.74
EUROPE:			ASIA:		
United Kingdom	1,033	9.01	Japan	67	
			Indonesia	187	
EUROPEAN ECONOMIC COMMUNITY: (excluding the U.K.)			Other	165	
			Sub-Total	419	3.66
			AFRICA:		
Belgium & Luxembourg	52		Republic of South Africa	126	
France	217		Other	52	
Italy	49		Sub-Total	178	1.55
Netherlands	110		AUSTRALASIA:		
West Germany	151				
Denmark	60		Australia	478	
Ireland	71		Other	34	
Sub-Total	710	6.20	Sub-Total	512	4.47
TOTAL Developed Countries	11,460 8,714	76.04	Developing Countries	2,746	23.96

Source: *Statistics Canada Daily*, (Catalogue 11-001E), 11 April 1979, p. 5.

Four key observations can be made with respect to CDIA: first, most of it was located in the *developed* world, that is, in members of the Organization for Economic Cooperation and Development (OECD). Second, the United States with more than one-half of the total was the major geographical area of concentration. In these respects, the territorial distribution of CDIA reflected the general pattern of Canadian international trade; during 1976 and 1978, approximately 70% of total Canadian exports and imports were with the United States, while nearly 90% involved members of the OECD (see Table 3). Third, the manu-

Table 2

CANADIAN DIRECT INVESTMENT ABROAD BY INDUSTRIAL DISTRIBUTION IN 1976 ($MILLIONS)

	U.S.	U.K.	All Other Countries	Total
Manufacturing:				
Beverages	797	237	240	1,274
Non-Ferrous metals	886	209	543	1,638
Wood and paper products	756	122	132	1,010
Iron and products	332	171	579	1,082
Chemicals and allied products	247	3	50	300
Other manufacturing	200	11	55	266
Sub-Total	3,218	753	1,599	5,570
Merchandising	182	37	196	415
Mining and Smelting	521	1	683	1,205
Petroleum and Natural Gas	1,073	110	224	1,407
Utilities	483	33	1,075	1,591
Financial	381	86	507	974
Other	194	13	91	298
TOTAL	6,052	1,033	4,375	11,460

Source: *Statistics Canada Daily*, (Catalogue 11-001E), 11 April 1979, p. 4.

In 1976, U.S. sources showed Canada having $5.9 billion U.S. of direct investment in the U.S., at a time when the two currencies were fluctuating around parity with each other. According to U.S. sources, 57% of the Canadian investment was in manufacturing, 12% in trade, 11% in petroleum, 5% in insurance and 15% in real estate and other: see, U.S. Department of Commerce, *Survey of Current Business*, (Aug. 1979), p. 46. At the end of 1978, the U.S. was host to $40.8 billion U.S. of foreign direct investment, equivalent to about $47.5 billion Canadian, compared to foreign investment in Canada of $49.5 Canadian. *Ibid.*, p. 38 for U.S. and Statistics Canada estimates for Canada.

facturing sector was the prime area for such investment, with much of it centred in the United States. Fourth, approximately nine-tenths of CDIA was held in subsidiaries which were 100% owned by the Canadian parent company.[2]

Two further observations should be noted. First, Canadian investment abroad, by non-Canadian controlled firms, had accounted for a notable, but steadily declining, proportion of CDIA. Because of the extensive foreign ownership of Canadian firms, some so-called Canadian companies investing abroad were actually owned and/or controlled from other countries, such as the Ford Motor Company of Canada. In some instances, the foreign owned Canadian multinational functioned as a fully integrated regional operation, while in other cases, tax and political convenience may have influenced the foreign parent to use the Canadian subsidiary as a base for investing abroad, without having delegated any of the management responsibilities for overseeing the activities of these *Canadian* subsidiaries.

Table 3

GEOGRAPHIC DISTRIBUTION OF CANADIAN INTERNATIONAL TRADE IN 1976, 1978 ($THOUSANDS)

Exports	1978	%	1976	%
United States	10,235,772	70.03	6,737,962	67.32
Japan	781,671	5.34	600,925	6.00
Britain	470,079	3.23	470,788	4.71
European Economic Community (excluding Britain)	881,626	6.03	789,021	7.88
Other O.E.C.D.	331,354	2.27	269,093	2.69
Other	1,914,793	13.10	1,141,113	11.40
Total	14,615,295	100.00	10,008,902	100.00
Imports				
United States	35,011,829	70.47	25,751,661	68.77
Japan	2,264,882	4.56	1,523,886	4.07
Britain	1,597,698	3.22	1,149,744	3.07
European Economic Community (excluding Britain)	3,031,814	6.10	1,990,969	5.32
Other O.E.C.D.	1,465,016	2.95	1,231,185	3.29
Other	6,312,759	12.70	5,796,944	15.48
Total	49,683,998	100.00	37,444,389	100.00

Sources: Statistics Canada, *Exports by Countries, January-December, 1978,* (Cat. 65-003), (Ottawa, 1979), p. 11; Statistics Canada, *Imports by Countries, January-December, 1978,* (Cat. 65-006), (Ottawa, 1979), p. 13.

While 37% of CDIA in 1969 was by firms controlled abroad, by 1974 this proportion had decreased to 19%.[3] During 1969, 90% of CDIA in Asia was by Canadian firms which were foreign controlled (and 10% by Canadian companies domestically controlled). Comparable figures for Australasia were 80%, South and Central America 75%, Africa 60%, Europe 40%, and North America less than 30%.[4] As shown in Table 4, by 1974, 18% of CDIA in Asia was by Canadian companies controlled from other countries, 57% for Australasia, 13% for Europe, and 1% for South and Central America.

The decline of the foreign controlled component of CDIA since 1969 may be attributed to three factors. Investment abroad has been undertaken by more Canadian based and controlled enterprises, both large and small; and some of the previously non-Canadian controlled companies have acquired the status of *Canadian* controlled firms, because of a change in their ownership composition and/or by virtue of a reclassification of their status by Canada's Foreign Investment Review Agency.

Table 4

CANADIAN DIRECT INVESTMENT ABROAD BY LOCATION OF INVESTMENT AND NATIONALITY OF CONTROL IN 1974 ($MILLIONS)

Location of Investment	Canada	%	All Foreign Countries	%	All Countries
NORTH AMERICA					
United States	3,951	80.48	958	19.52	4,909
Mexico	52	83.87	10	16.13	62
Bahamas	135	74.59	46	25.41	181
Bermuda	309	72.88	115	27.12	424
Jamaica	100	95.24	5	4.76	105
Trinidad & Tabago	13	72.22	5	27.78	18
Other	33	33.33	66	66.67	99
Sub-Total	4,593	79.22	1,205	20.78	5,798
SOUTH AND CENTRAL AMERICA					
Venezuela					16
Argentina	991	99.10	9	0.90	33
Brazil					951
Other	70	93.33	5	6.67	75
Sub-Total	1,061	98.70	14	1.30	1,075
EUROPE					
United Kingdom	781	88.85	98	11.15	879
EUROPEAN ECONOMIC COMMUNITY (EXCLUDING U.K.)					
Belgium & Luxembourg	23	62.16	14	37.84	37
France	169	100.00	—	0.00	169
Italy	35	94.59	2	5.41	37
Netherlands	38	88.37	5	11.63	43
West Germany	106	84.80	19	15.20	125
Denmark	39	97.50	1	2.50	40
Ireland	16	25.40	47	74.60	63
Sub-Total EEC	426	82.88	88	17.12	514
Switzerland	85	98.84	1	1.16	86
Norway					59
Spain	117	83.57	23	16.43	35
Other					46
Sub-Total Europe	1,409	87.03	210	12.97	1,619
AFRICA					
Reb. of South Africa	34	31.19	75	68.81	109
Other	9	28.13	23	71.87	32
Sub-Total	43	30.50	98	69.50	141

Location of Investment	Canada	%	All Foreign Countries	%	All Countries
ASIA					
Japan	75	97.40	2	2.60	77
Other	120	74.07	42	15.93	162
Sub-Total	195	81.59	44	18.41	239
AUSTRALASIA					
Australia	173	43.47	225	56.53	398
Other	13	35.14	24	64.86	37
Sub-Total	186	42.76	249	57.24	435
TOTAL	7,487	80.44	1,820	19.56	9,307
Developed Countries	5,620	79.02	1,492	20.98	7,112
Developing Countries	1,867	85.06	328	14.94	2,195

Source: *Statistics Canada, Canada's International Investment Position 1974*, (Cat. 67-202), (Ottawa, 1976), p. 54.

Statistics Canada has indicated that the proportion of investments in manufacturing industries in Canada, which were domestically controlled, increased from 40% to 44% between 1969 and 1975, and in mining industries from 30% to 40%.[5] It is reasonable to expect this trend to continue, since there were net decreases in the amount of foreign capital directly invested in Canada during 1976 and 1978.[6] Some foreign-controlled enterprises have been acquired by domestic firms, such as Husky Oil by Alberta Gas Trunk Line, or by crown corporations, such as Texasgulf by the Canadian Development Corporation and Pacific Petroleum by Petro-Canada. These changes are significant, since the implications for Canada of the foreign controlled component of CDIA may differ from that of CDIA which is domestically controlled.

Finally, CDIA is highly concentrated in a few large enterprises. Statistics Canada revealed in 1974 that 16 large Canadian enterprises accounted for about 67% of total CDIA. Based on data collected by the authors, this figure may in fact understate the already high level of concentration of CDIA in a handful of *Canadian* based and controlled enterprises (see Table 5).

The data obtained by the authors differ significantly from the totals compiled by Statistics Canada. The previously noted $11.5 billion of CDIA, as of 1976, has been compiled on the basis of flows and claims between all Canadian parent companies and their foreign subsidiaries. The data surveyed and compiled by the authors include all corporate assets located abroad, including those foreign held assets acquired through local (foreign) financing. The difference between the balance of payments calculation of direct investment and that of overseas corporate assets is best demonstrated in a benchmark study of foreign direct

Table 5

CANADIAN DIRECT INVESTMENT ABROAD BY AREA OF CONTROL AND SIZE OF INVESTMENT, 1974 ($MILLIONS)

Size of investment abroad by Canadian enterprises controlled in Canada:	Number of Enterprises	$M	% of Total
Over $50 million	17	6,038	64.9
Between $25 and $50 million	14	478	5.1
Between $10 and $25 million	28	443	4.8
Less than $10 million	526	528	5.7
Sub-Total	585	7,487	80.5
All Foreign countries:			
Over $50 million	8	799	8.6
Between $25 and $50 million	9	319	3.4
Between $10 and $25 million	23	382	4.1
Less than $10 million	304	320	3.4
Sub-Total	344	1,820	19.5
All countries:			
Over $100 million	16	6,230	66.9
Between $50 and $100 million	9	607	6.5
Between $25 and $50 million	23	797	8.6
Between $10 and $25 million	51	825	8.9
Between $5 and $10 million	43	319	3.4
Between $1 and $5 million	183	425	4.6
Less than $1 million	604	104	1.1
Total	929	9,307	100.00

Source: Statistics Canada, *Canada's International Investment Position 1974,* (Ottawa, 1976), p. 56.

investment in the United States.[7] At year end 1973, the U.S. government estimated that Canada's direct investment position in the United States was $5.2 billion U.S., compared to $3.9 billion U.S. estimated by Statistics Canada, while the balance sheet assets of Canada's U.S. affiliates, according to the U.S. study, totalled in the neighbourhood of $24 billion U.S. Total asset data needs to be collected in order to examine the full public policy implications of CDIA. For example, related to the U.S. assets figure for Canada, 175,973 people were employed by the U.S. affiliates of Canadian based companies.[8]

THE CORPORATE LANDSCAPE

Canada is atypical among industrialized nations because so much of its industry is owned and controlled by foreign investors. This phenomenon can be quickly gleaned by examining *The Financial Post* top 200 industrial Canadian companies ranked by sales for 1978/79. Of the 200 companies,

> 71 are wholly owned by foreign parent companies, 38 are 50% or more owned, and there are another 19 where there is substantial, sometimes controlling, foreign interests.[9]

About 75% of these 128 firms have their headquarters in the United States.

A commonly accepted definition of a multinational enterprise is one that has "controlled manufacturing subsidiaries in six or more countries."[10] The parent companies of most of these large foreign controlled Canadian firms meet this condition, and the majority of them are either listed on the *Fortune 500* Largest U.S. or non-U.S. Industrial Corporations.

Canada has 39 firms on the *Fortune 1976* list of the "500 Largest Non-U.S. Industrial Corporations"; however, only 22 of these firms are Canadian controlled, and they form the basis of this study of CDIA. The Canadian contingent is listed by sales, assets and employees in Table 6. The leading Canadian-owned firm is Massey-Ferguson which ranked 80th on this *Fortune* list, and was a distant fifth to General Motors of Canada which ranked 32nd. General Motors of Canada had sales of approximately $5.3 billion in 1976, almost twice the total of Massey-Ferguson, and it was the first company in Canada to exceed the $5 billion sales figure. The other non-Canadian controlled companies whose sales exceeded Massey-Ferguson were as follows (in rank order): Ford Motor of Canada, Imperial Oil and Chrysler Canada.

To what extent are Canadian controlled firms multinational? Based on the Harvard criteria of "manufacturing subsidiaries in six or more countries", many of the *Group of 22* could not be considered multinational. On the other hand, if the criteria were altered to include firms which operate subsidiaries in at least two foreign countries, then most of these firms could be viewed as multinational.

Rather than formulate a convenient criterion to fit the *Group of 22*, the authors conducted a short survey in 1977 to ascertain the companies' geographic breakdown of sales, assets and employees for 1975/76 (see Table 6). In the case of Canadian Pacific Investments, a holding company, data were obtained for two of its more important subsidiaries—Cominco and Algoma. The following observations could be made concerning the overseas operations of all these firms.

Sales — In the case of nine companies, non-Canadian sales exceeded sales in Canada as a percentage of total corporate sales. Some of the comparisons were quite extreme, for example, Massey-Ferguson 92% vs. 8%; Alcan 83% vs. 17%; Seagram 94% vs. 6%, Inco 89% vs. 11%; Moore 90% vs. 10%; and Hiram Walker 88% vs. 12%. In every case, U.S. corporate sales equalled or exceeded company sales in Canada. Five of the

Table 6

CANADIAN CONTROLLED COMPANIES ON THE FORTUNE LIST OF LARGEST NON-U.S. INDUSTRIAL CORPORATIONS 1976
GEOGRAPHIC DISTRIBUTION OF SALES, ASSETS, & EMPLOYEES

Company	Sales Total ($000)	Can.	U.S.	U.K.	Other	Assets Total ($000)	Can.	U.S.	U.K.	Other	Employees Total	Can.	U.S.	U.K.	Other
		---- % ----					---- % ----					---- % ----			
Massey-Ferguson	2,771,696	8	23	8	61	2,305,145	11	26	15	48	68,200	12	9	17	62
Alcan Aluminum	2,656,072	17	21	15	47	3,090,239	48	9	16	27	60,000	31	6	14	49
Canadian Pacific Investments*	2,152,259	- - - N.A. - - -				4,046,339	- - - N.A. - - -				36,948	- - - N.A. - - -			
Seagram	2,048,970	6	68	--26--		2,161,193	10	- 90**-			17,000	10	- 90** -		
Inco	2,040,282	11	50	12	27	3,628,311	53	23	9	15	55,767	46	27	15	12
Canada Packers	1,609,089	85	4	4	7	314,975	82	3	5	10	15,000	79	1	6	14
MacMillan Bloedel	1,542,022	24	45	9	22	1,268,155	61	23	13	3	23,601	77	15	7	1
Steel Co. of Canada	1,379,642	88	8	--4--		1,823,723	96	4	—		22,691	99	1	—	
Noranda Mines	1,250,079	25	25	7.5	42.5	2,073,207	75	12.5	—	12.5	32,649	85	7.5	—	7.5
Northern Telecom	1,127,966	86	9	--5--		698,482	80	15	--5--		25,277	80	12	--8--	
Moore	1,053,241	10	63	7	20	764,262	9	61	11	19	25,964	9	51	15	25
Dominion Foundries	916,845	90	5	1	4	1,023,543	98	2	—	—	11,500	100	—	—	—
Genstar	901,097	80	18	—	2	1,221,378	85	12	—	3	10,695	89	10	—	1
Domtar	899,494	78	15	7	—	760,763	94	3	3	—	17,520	93	2	5	—
Abitibi	892,984	40	48	--12--		891,000	78	22	—	—	22,000	91	9	—	—
Consolidated Bathurst	755,887	55	20	5	20	735,760	90	—	—	10	17,557	85	—	—	15
Burns Foods	732,178	95	2	—	3	162,425	100	—	—	—	6,971	100	—	—	—
John Labatt	683,336	93	6	--1--		446,626	90	5	--5--		12,150	95	5	—	—
Molson	663,015	96	3	1	—	428,063	95	4	1	—	10,695	97	2	1	—
Dominion Bridge	543,994	67	33	—	—	357,270	60	40	—	—	10,313	55	45	—	—
Hiram-Walker	543,955	12	58	3	27	912,388	16	33	25	26	7,500	25	23	24	28
Dominion Textile	472,915	60	25	3	12	360,702	69	21	1	9	13,130	79	18	—	3
Cominco*	725,005	25	39	16	20	973,205	63	18	1.5	17.5	10,696	80	9	.5	10.5
Algoma Steel*	584,835	78	21	--1--		928,248	89	11	—	—	12,200	91	9	—	—

*Cominco and Algoma Steel are controlled by Canadian Pacific Investments Limited (CPI) which in turn is a subsidiary of Canadian Pacific Limited.

**Largely in the U.S.

Source: *Fortune*, Vol. 96 (August 1977), and Company Survey.

nine companies had non-Canadian sales in excess of $1 billion: Massey-Ferguson, Alcan, Seagram, Inco and MacMillan Bloedel.

Assets — Unlike the sales situation, only a few companies held a majority of their assets outside Canada; Massey-Ferguson, Alcan, Seagram, Moore and Hiram-Walker. Other companies with significant assets abroad were Inco (47%), MacMillan Bloedel (39%), Noranda (25%), Northern Telecom (20%), Abitibi (22%), Dominion Bridge (40%), and Dominion Textile (31%). Cominco, a subsidiary of Canadian Pacific Investments, had 37% of its corporate assets abroad. In the case of Massey-Ferguson, Seagram, and Moore, U.S. corporate assets exceeded the Canadian totals.

The corporate process of internationalization has moved more rapidly in the functional area of marketing (sales) than in assets. This may be attributed to a combination of the following reasons: first, extended and extensive exporting of goods from Canada is often a precursor to undertaking substantial investments abroad; second, Canadian controlled firms in manufacturing are relatively late entrants as multinationals, compared to their European and U.S. counterparts; and, third, many of these firms are in resource based industries, are highly capital intensive in Canada, and until recently, were largely export-oriented.

This scenario is changing as more Canadian companies are vertically integrating forwards, and diversifying their operations through foreign acquisitions and the formation of new establishments abroad. As of 1976, four Canadian companies had corporate assets in excess of one billion dollars located outside Canada; namely, Massey-Ferguson, Alcan, Seagram, and Inco. Moreover, these firms were among the more aggressive Canadian companies currently expanding abroad.

Employees — As one might expect, the distribution of employees paralleled the geographic breakdown of corporate assets. In addition to Massey-Ferguson, Alcan, Seagram, Moore and Hiram-Walker, Inco had more employees working for the corporation abroad than in Canada (54% vs. 46%). Generally speaking, these six companies were the most internationally diverse of the *Group of 22*. A key characteristic of Canadian multinationals is that the domestic market declines rapidly in importance as they internationalize their operations, and the contribution of Canadian sales to total corporate (global) sales drops significantly behind the U.S. figures.

As previously noted, four Canadian companies, Massey-Ferguson, Alcan, Seagram and Inco, have overseas assets valued in excess of $1 billion each. These may be viewed as members of the Canadian billion dollar club when dealing with CDIA. Brascan, a Toronto-based firm, could also satisfy the billion dollar criterion. Until 1978, it was primarily a regulated utility distributing company, and was excluded from the

Fortune list. At that time, Brascan could be described as a binational firm, Canada and Brazil — with most of its operations based in Brazil. Another potential club member was Bata Shoes, a privately-held corporation, with headquarters in Toronto. Most of Bata's activities and investments were also based abroad, but unlike Brascan, they were geographically diverse. Bata had operating subsidiaries in 90 countries, 58% of its assets were located in less developed economies, and only 3% of its global sales were realized in Canada.

INTERNATIONALIZING THE DOMESTIC OPERATION

Why do Canadian firms invest abroad? In an interview with executives of Canada Packers Limited, the following reasons were offered:

1. *Growth* — The Canadian market is small, and its growth potential is limited relative to the rest of the world whose standard of living is rapidly increasing.
2. *Tariff and Non-Tariff Barriers* — Specifically, trading blocs such as the European Economic Community tend to limit the scope for direct exporting through quotas and health regulations.
3. *Sources of Supply* — Canada alone does not have a large enough surplus of lamb and beef to allow the firm to capitalize on the many profitable opportunities that are identifiable in the global market place.
4. *Defensive Marketing* — Establishing overseas subsidiaries not only provides access to new markets but, in addition, such action may dissuade a local firm from exporting to Canada.
5. *Transportation* — Distant and affluent markets can often be more profitably serviced from overseas affiliates, for example, exporting to the Japanese market from the Australian affiliate.

Canada Packers produces a full line of packing house products and by-products. The company also handles other farm products, in addition to canning certain foods and processing leather. In 1976, Canada Packers' consolidated sales approximated $1.6 billion, and 15% of this total was realized through its overseas operations which include wholly and partially owned subsidiaries in the United States, United Kingdom, Australia, Germany and Mexico. In addition, the company maintained marketing subsidiaries and trading agencies in the major geographical markets of the world.

Canada Packers exhibited certain corporate characteristics common to many large Canadian-owned firms which had *gone international* but had yet to achieve a *multinational* status. These characteristics included the following: corporate sales and assets were largely concentrated in the North American market; the companies were recent entrants in the field of global investment and business, as distinct from North American business; and there was usually a structural division between domestic and international business activities, with the latter divided between exporting and operating subsidiaries. Exporting may be handled through a trading division or company, and the foreign subsidiaries may report either to a senior vice-president, or, depending upon the importance of their operations, directly to the president.

Most of the firms in Table 6 were undergoing various degrees of internationalization. The experience of some of these firms, particularly the ones which had achieved a multinational status, will now be examined in the context of the key motivational factors which promote the growth of multinational business.

Need For Command Over Vital Resources

Companies in the extractive industries may find themselves pressured to become multinational, because major ore deposits are not to be found in Canada, or because of insufficient domestic supplies. The growth and operations of Alcan Aluminium Limited is one such example. In international terms, Canada ranks among the major world producers in 16 of 17 key minerals. The notable exception is bauxite, the basic aluminum ore, which is absent in Canada. This fact is all the more significant since Canada is the world's fourth largest producer of primary aluminum, and Alcan is one of the world's leading manufacturers of primary aluminum and its related products.

Unlike Canada Packers, Alcan is heavily dependent on its overseas operations, measured in terms of capital employed and in sales of aluminum. In 1976, 52% of the company's fixed capital was outside of Canada, and 83% of sales was realized in foreign markets. In addition, more than two-thirds of the approximately 60,000 Alcan employees worked outside Canada. On January 1, 1968, Nathaniel Davis, the President of Alcan, announced a company reorganization, pointing to factors of absolute size, geographical diversity, and increased vertical integration as the prime considerations.

The company saw the need for reorganization as a result of internal and external pressures:

> Not only had the company itself changed — from essentially a basic metal manufacturer to increasingly a leading producer of semi-fabricated and finished products — but so had the world in which it lived. Communications were faster, markets were different, competition was intensified.[11]

Though significant, the move was by no means pathbreaking, nor were the circumstances leading to it unique to Alcan. A survey of 170 U.S. multinational companies showed that, by 1968, only eight of the companies had not made this or some similar move.[12] The basic characteristic of reorganization was to move from a highly centralized staff-functional to a more decentralized product-line structure.

Access to Foreign Markets

Canadian based multinationals stress that, to remain competitive in most export markets, will usually oblige them to consider investing in local manufacturing and sales operations. The reasons offered are two-fold: first, at the macro level, most foreign governments, like Canada, pursue a myriad of import substitution and export promotion policies designed to foster local manufacturing activity. When such activity is apparent, other market barriers are usually introduced to favour the local manufacturer over foreign suppliers. Elements of such policies usually include tariffs, fiscal incentives, and non-tariff barriers, including government procurement guidelines, which tend to discriminate against foreign suppliers.

At the micro level, the successful Canadian exporter may decide to establish an overseas operation because of increasing competition faced from domestic (local) manufacturing, including the prospect of another foreign supplier establishing an affiliate in that market. Transportation costs, problems of servicing local customers, and the opportunities of pursuing product differentiation strategies unique to the export market, are some of the other factors which may influence the decision to invest abroad.

An excellent example of a Canadian multinational enterprise which has responded to, as well as having initiated, pressures for internationalizing its manufacturing and marketing operations is Massey-Ferguson Limited. One of the interesting features of Massey-Ferguson's corporate strategy is its international production strategy which promotes a policy of maximum interchangeability of component parts, especially for tractors and combines. This policy appears to reduce the costs of production by having factories situated in different countries specializing in different models at differing levels of production.[13]

The fact that almost every country in the world constitutes a potential market for Massey-Ferguson products means that corporate management must make decisions on a world-wide basis. This is particularly so, since Massey-Ferguson has major investment commitments abroad, a product line that can be merchandised in a series of markets, and a product line of interchangeable parts which can be supplied from several production bases. A major benefit of the foregoing strategy is that management can shift sources of supply for a given market from one country to another, in response to differing governmental and non-governmental policies and pressures, such as dividend restrictions or work stoppages caused by militant union elements in a particular country.

Massey-Ferguson has also pioneered in the area of joint east/west industrial cooperation. For example, in September, 1974, Massey-Ferguson entered into an agreement with a Polish enterprise to assist in the expansion and modernization of the Polish tractor industry. Under this agreement, Poland was acquiring Massey-Ferguson technology leading to the annual production of 75,000 Massey-Ferguson tractors and 90,000 Perkins engines. Initially, Massey-Ferguson would export a substantial volume of parts and engines to produce these products, with the long run objective of utilizing certain Polish manufactured components in its own manufacturing operations, as well as in marketing Polish-made goods through its distribution channels. The joint East-West Cooperation Agreement was but another way of achieving access to foreign markets, where legislation may prevent foreign companies from establishing their own operations, without sacrificing the advantages of international specialization of labour, and the attendant benefits in the areas of production and sales.

Market Saturation And The Drive For Growth

The Canadian market is small, relative to the United States, the European Economic Community and Japan. Expanding the size of its market has been a major factor underlying the growth of the multinational enterprise. The larger and more successful Canadian firms have found it necessary to expand overseas in order to achieve both plant and firm economies of scale. These firms also contend that market size and share are pre-requisite conditions for supporting a managerial and technological capability, which allows them to compete against foreign multinationals in Canada and abroad. A common statement from the management of these firms is that investing in foreign market development provides a higher return than the one realized from achieving a marginal improvement in the Canadian market. This statement is most apparent where the Canadian firm enjoys a substantial portion of the Canadian market. Attributing the foreign investment decision to the fear of attracting the attention of Canadian anti-combines authorities appears to be of secondary importance.

One of the unique features of prominent Canadian multinationals is that the domestic market declines rapidly in importance, as the firm internationalizes its operations. This fact may be measured in terms of sales, assets, and employment (see Table 6). For many of the Canadian multinationals, the domestic market, as a percentage of total corporate sales, is considerably less important than the U.S. market. Many large Canadian firms with overseas investments tend to depend on the U.S. market for their survival and success. In fact, their new product diversification programs are often predicated on their anticipated ability to achieve market success in the United States.

Canadian firms which go international often establish their first foreign subsidiary in the U.S., not unlike many U.S. multinationals which have incorporated their first foreign affiliate in Canada. However, the similarity stops at this point, because the Canadian market seldom occupies a position of critical importance to the U.S. firm. To take an extreme example, Moore Corporation Limited was formed in Toronto in 1882 and established its first foreign affiliate in Niagara Falls, N.Y. in 1884. By 1974, the U.S. market accounted for 63% of total corporate sales, and both the research and marketing divisions of the corporation were based in New York.

The heavy dependence on the U.S. market has a profound effect on a Canadian company's corporate strategy and structure. The geographical proximity between the Canadian head office and the U.S. subsidiary, and the similarity in language and management philosophy, promote ease of communication between the two parts of the corporation. The same phenomenon holds true between the head office organization of a U.S. firm and its subsidiary in Canada. In the case of the latter example, the Canadian division is sometimes viewed as an appendage of the U.S. organization, or as a division in the North American geographical region, which is largely dependent on the U.S. corporate infrastructure. The situation is different when the head office is located in Canada. The similarities between the two countries, coupled with the size of the U.S. market, promotes a situation where market size suggests that the U.S. subsidiary will enjoy far greater power *vis à vis* the parent, to the point that critical parts of the corporate infrastructure are based in the U.S., servicing both the U.S. divisions, as well as the Canadian part of the operation.

Relative Scarcity of Productivity Factors

The factors of production include land (including raw materials), labour, capital, and intermediate products. In the case of capital, one includes financial and human capital. The latter component may involve skilled labour, managerial talent and entrepreneurship. Countries possess different proportions of factors of production, and a company is faced with the need to judge the relative costs associated with establishing the unit of production in different locations. The *scarcities* of the different factors are continuously being altered as a result of inflationary forces, tariffs, changes in tax, foreign exchange fluctuations, wage agreements, and other forms of government intervention.

The U.S.-Canadian situation is a good example of the foregoing point. The comparative labour cost advantage traditionally enjoyed by Canada over the U.S. was gradually eliminated during the 1970s. Since labour costs in the manufacturing sector approximate 70% of the final costs, this comparison acquires added significance for the Canadian firm in deciding whether to expand its Canadian operation, or to invest in the establishment, or expansion, of an American base of operation.

Tax and Other Financial Advantages

Governments, especially those in developing countries, pursue policies aimed at encouraging multinationals to establish overseas manufacturing operations in their countries. These policies usually consist of tax holidays, customs exemptions, financial subsidies, loans, or special tariff treatment. In some instances, the governments of developed countries, such as Canada, also offer incentives of their own to encourage their firms to establish overseas operations in the third world. A Canadian firm may find an initially unattractive investment to be commercially profitable, by virtue of tax and other financial advantages offered by both the parent (Canadian) government and the prospective host government. A good case in point involves the Reliable Toy Company Limited of Toronto.

This company received financial assistance from the Canadian International Development Agency (CIDA) when it first explored the feasibility of establishing an overseas subsidiary in the Caribbean. One of CIDA's goals is to promote Canadian investment in developing countries. It does this by providing a $2,500 grant for a *starter* study, which is designed to assist the Canadian investor to make an on the spot assessment. This can be followed with a grant of up to $25,000 for a feasibility study on a shared cost basis (50/50) with the potential investor. Apparently, this incentive spurred Reliable Toy to investigate the potential market opportunity in Jamaica. The net result of this study was the establishment of a joint-venture arrangement in 1973 between Reliable Toy and a local Jamaican firm, split 60/40 in favor of Reliable. This joint venture received a tax holiday for five years from the Jamaican government, was permitted to import the necessary machinery duty-free, and could import some of the critical materials, such as resins, at a preferred rate of duty. Moreover, the joint-venture received a rebate on customs duty on toys exported to Canada.

Not all incentives need be initiated by governments. As companies internationalize their operations and increase intra-corporate trade, the technique of transfer pricing offers attractive opportunities for pricing the movement of goods and services between different countries in ways which take advantage of different tax jurisdictions. The most common example is to have the low tax affiliate sell high and buy low in non-arms length transactions. Pricing management and research services at unrealistic rates is another way of repatriating funds between jurisdictions whose level of taxation may differ. Tax havens in such countries as Switzerland, Lichtenstein, Monaco, Bermuda and the Bahamas, simply help to promote and perpetuate *dummy* trading companies and subsidiary/ head-office configurations, which have little resemblance to the actual economic activities of these operations. Canadian multinationals are not unique in employing tax havens and other fiscal arrangements to their advantage.

Not all of these manoeuvres are entirely successful, and the example of Dominion Bridge Ltd. may be taken as a case in point.[14] Incorporated in 1882, and reorganized in 1912 under Dominion charter, Dominion Bridge currently has plants in seven Canadian provinces, about a dozen subsidiaries in the U.S., as well as operations in the Bahamas and Belgium; its products are sold or installed in 75 countries. The firm produces and distributes steel, and undertakes the design, fabrication and erection of steel in construction and industrial equipment goods.

Dominion Bridge purchases approximately 85% of its steel from domestic market sources in Canada and the United States, with the balance derived from off-shore mills, either directly or through an agent or broker designated by the foreign supplier. The agents receive a commission of about 3%, and the purchaser does not know the precise mill price which is charged to the agent or broker.

During the 1960s, the different affiliated operations of Dominion Bridge had virtually complete freedom of action in their steel purchases and often failed to provide information from one branch to another. Thus, some plants had large steel supplies, while others suffered from shortages, a chaotic and expensive situation, given the frequently slow turnover of inventories. Management directed that all off-shore purchases should be controlled by the head office in the most profitable manner, that is, by eliminating the use of agents via direct negotiations with foreign suppliers and by minimizing the tax costs of business operations.

In April, 1966, a subsidiary, Span International, was incorporated in the Bahamas.

> To prospect for and to contract with others to prospect and search for sources of raw steel supplies in any and every part of the world and to enter into contracts with others for the supply of raw steel and allied raw materials and allied products.
>
> To carry on the business of Commission Agents, Manufacturers' Agents, Importers, Exporters, Insurance Agents, Merchant Bankers, and General Merchants.[15]

Span International was capitalized at £350 into one thousand shares with a par value of seven shillings each. The directors of Span could confer upon a Director holding executive office, any of the powers of the firm "with restrictions as they think fit."

No employee of Span had any background in steel purchasing, and the work was managed by officers of a trust company in Nassau, after instructions were received from employees of Domionion Bridge under the close scrutiny of a vice-president, who was either a director or was present at the meetings of the directors. Contracts with foreign mills were made by Dominion Bridge employees. During 1968 and 1969, the president of Span was replaced by a retired officer of the parent firm. A junior executive, who used to be an officer of its purchasing department, was sent to look after various aspects of Span's activities, but without policy-making responsibilities, although he retained the title of manager.

The manager of Span had no leeway at all in the purchase of offshore steel, but had to follow procedures set down by the vice-president of Dominion Bridge. When he travelled to Europe and Japan, he was accompanied by an executive of the parent operation, and could not commit Span to any contract without the approval of the vice-president. Span paid the off-shore price for foreign steel, but Dominion Bridge paid Span up to 95% of the domestic steel price for that steel. The steel was shipped directly to Dominion Bridge, with all documents being written at its head office and copies forwarded to Span.

In an appeal of Dominion Bridge against a ruling by the Ministry of National Revenue, it was found in the Federal Court of Canada in 1975, that Dominion Bridge had willfully violated the Income Tax Act for the taxation years of 1967, 1968 and 1969. Judge Décary noted that:

> In causing Span to be incorporated the Appellant was in fact going to put aside part of its profits in the hands of Span for safe-keeping in a tax-free country and the Appellant could always repatriate these profits to Canada tax-free by virtue of section 28 of the Act.
>
> The problem is illuminated when one weighs the manner in which the profits were made. The Appellant paid Span 95% of the price of domestic steel, or 95% of the fair market value of domestic steel when in fact it should have paid Span the fair market value of off-shore steel. The off-shore steel of Span sold to the Appellant did not become domestic by the mere fact that a copy of the relevant papers was sent by the off-shore mills to Span at Nassau.
>
> The difference between the fair market value of off-shore steel and the fair market value of domestic steel permitted Span to make about 18% profit, which profit would have been made by the Appellant if it had paid the market value of off-shore steel in lieu of the market value of domestic steel. The Appellant chose to pay Span 95% of the price of domestic steel for off-shore steel and thereby increased its costs of purchases by 18% that being the profit margin of Span.[16]

Dominion Bridge argued that Span was a valid legal entity, which was separate from it in law, and in fact, that it was a non-resident of Canada and a resident of the Bahamas, and that it had never been an agent of Dominion Bridge. Judge Décary described this so-called separate relationship as a "sham." The control of Span was so detailed that it was "a puppet of the Appellant"; Dominion Bridge was in effect "the directing mind and will" of Span. The expenses and disbursements which Dominion Bridge made to create and operate Span, as well as Span's income from interest and dividends, were merely "feigned" as the costs and income of Span.

Dominion Bridge was found guilty of overstating its cost of sales for 1967, 1968 and 1969 by $3.15 million. Also added back to its income, were

$358 thousand in alleged legal, appraisal, and audit fees, bad debts and commission expenses incurred by Dominion Bridge in its dealings with Span, and interest or dividend income of Span. Dominion Bridge's appeal was dismissed with legal and court costs.

THE BILLION DOLLAR CLUB[17]

Alcan and Aluminum

In the Western world, six large multinational companies with vertically integrated operations control approximately 55% of the aluminum smelting capacity. These six producers are Alcan (Canada), Alcoa, Reynolds and Kaiser (U.S.), Pechiney (France), and Alusuisse (Switzerland).

Two of the characteristics of the North American industry are its dependence on imported sources of bauxite and/or alumina, which the major firms have traditionally owned or controlled, and the large number of independent fabricators that manufacture aluminum products, often in competition with the major producers. In Canada, these characteristics are accentuated even further. The Canadian aluminum industry is entirely dependent on imported bauxite; smelting capacity is owned 85% by Alcan and 15% by Canadian Reynolds; Canadian consumption of aluminum products is supplied about 68% by Alcan, 20% by Canadian Reynolds and 12% by imports and secondary aluminum. A very high proportion of aluminum produced is exported from Canada. Consequently, the Canadian aluminum industry can be closely identified with Alcan, and the livelihood of this industry can be seen to be very dependent on external factors.

Measured in terms of capital employed and sales of aluminum during 1976, 42% of Alcan's fixed capital was outside Canada, and 83% of sales were realized in foreign markets. In addition, 69% of the approximately 60,000 Alcan employees worked outside Canada.

> Alcan's subsidiary and related companies have bauxite holdings in seven countries, produce aluminum in six, smelt primary aluminum in ten, fabricate aluminum in thirty-four, have sales outlets in over one hundred, and maintain warehouse inventories in the larger market.[18]

Is Alcan a Canadian company? Many Canadians and foreigners alike perceive Alcan to be an American firm, not a Canadian company. However, judging by the criteria of registered ownership, location of headquarters organization, and nationality of senior management and the board of directors, Alcan is a Canadian multinational corporation. In mid-1976, the registered ownership of the more than 40 million shares of Alcan Aluminium Limited (the parent holding company), then outstanding, was 49.0% in Canada, 37.3% in the United States and 13.7% in other countries. Moreover, the majority of the directors and officers of Alcan were citizens of Canada. In 1976, the Canadian government, through the Foreign Investment Review Agency, classified Alcan as a Canadian company, not bound by its regulations governing acquisitions and new investments into related and unrelated areas of Canadian business activity by *foreign owned* firms.

The perception of Alcan as an American company has risen from the knowledge that its corporate roots were in the United States, and that there was majority U.S. ownership in the company until the late 1960s. At the turn of the century (July 3, 1902), the Aluminum Company of America (Alcoa) established a Canadian affiliate under the name of the Northern Aluminum Company, Limited. Some 23 years later, on July 8, 1925, the corporate name was altered to the Aluminum Company of Canada, Limited, hereafter referred to as Alcan Canada, which on May 31, 1928, became the principal operating subsidiary of Aluminium Limited, the holding company know as Alcan. This Canadian incorporated company was assigned all of Alcoa's foreign holdings, except for its bauxite operations in Surinam.

The first *corporate separation* between Alcoa and Alcan appeared to have been prompted more by managerial ambition, rather than possible U.S. antitrust action. Arthur Vining Davis was Chairman of the Board of Alcoa in 1928, when two of his subordinates were competing for the Presidency of the firm: Roy A. Hunt, son of Captain Alfred Hunt, a founding member of Alcoa, and E.K. Davis, Arthur's younger brother. The split between Alcoa and Alcan allowed A.V. Davis to appoint his brother, E.K. Davis, to the presidency of Alcan, while Alfred E. Hunt was named president of Alcoa.

On assuming the presidency of Alcan, E.K. Davis brought with him to Canada a small group of Alcoa-trained personnel, who collectively were responsible for the emergence of this company as a giant industrial enterprise in Canada. Some of the Alcoa-Alcan pioneers were visible and dominant in a number of the key managerial positions and boardrooms of Alcan, and its key operating subsidiary, Alcan Canada, up until the late 1960s.

Running parallel with the managerial changes, significant antitrust developments dramatically altered the U.S. ownership composition of Alcan, and its links to Alcoa. In April of 1937, the U.S. Department of Justice filed a complaint under the U.S. antitrust laws, naming as defendants, the Aluminium Company of America (Alcoa), 25 of its subsidiaries and affiliated companies, including Alcan and 37 of its directors, officers and shareholders. The complaint alleged that Alcoa monopolized the manufacture of virgin aluminum ingot, and the sale of aluminum sheets, alloys, bars, etc. in the United States. The case was formally ended 20 years later in 1957.

Although no wrongdoing was proven by the antitrust authorities, the court ordered in June of 1950 that the shareholders of Alcoa be required to dispose of their stock interests either in Alcan or Alcoa, to ensure the future competitiveness of the U.S. aluminum industry. All the principal shareholders, except E.K. Davis, elected to sell their Alcan shares, and by December, 1957, the disposition order, with a small balance of shares outstanding, was completed.

Alcan has grown rapidly, from a relatively small firm, to one of giant proportion, even in global terms — second only to Alcoa. The company's corporate thrust has changed from being chiefly a producer and exporter of primary aluminum to a large vertically integrated producer, which increasingly consumes its own primary aluminum output in its world-wide fabricating plants, producing a myriad of industrial and consumer goods manufactured from aluminum. A major ingredient for the success of this strategy rested on Alcan's investment and penetration of the U.S. market.

Alcan's U.S. subsidiary, Alcan Aluminum Corporation (Alcancorp), which was nothing more than a sales subsidiary in 1944, emerged as the fourth largest aluminum fabricator in the United States, and its sales in 1976 would have easily placed it on the *Fortune* list of the 500 largest industrial corporations in the United States.

The importance of Alcan's U.S. subsidiary cannot be underesti-mated: in 1976, sales to third parties in the United States accounted for about 21% of Alcan's total worldwide sales, and for approximately 9% of Alcan's total capital employed. Similarly, the importance of Alcancorp's contribution to Alcan Canada, and hence its impact on Canada, cannot be overemphasized: "approximately 75% of U.S. ingot imports comes from Alcan and 80% from Canada as a whole."[19] As a result of Alcan's investment into fabrication in the United States, there was a very high degree of corporate interdependence and integration between Alcan Canada and Alcancorp. This explains why Alcan actively encouraged the creation of a North American free trade arrangement, at least in primary aluminum.

In recent years, the shape of a new corporate strategy appears to be emerging; a strategy that will not necessarily be linked to the require-ments of Alcan Canada, that is, consumption of largely Canadian produced primary aluminum. In 1971, David M. Culver, currently Chief Executive Officer of Alcan Canada, projected a scenario in which Canadian smelter production would be geared essentially to North American requirements, especially those of the United States, and would play a marginal role as a supplier to other foreign markets.

Traditionally, competitive pressures have led Alcan to erect local smelting operations (abroad), in order to protect its dominant local position. Currently, in order to enter certain new markets or retain its position in existing markets, Alcan is being pressured into establishing fully integrated aluminum industries (self-contained ingot and fabricating systems), even in those countries where the importation of Canadian primary aluminum might make the venture more efficient. These investments are being made because of their strategic and economic importance to the general competitiveness of Alcan as a multinational enterprise, of which Alcan Canada is one part, albeit a critical one.

Inco and Nickel

Inco is the world's largest producer of nickel, a substantial producer of copper, which is associated with nickel in the nickel-bearing sulphide ore mines in Canada, and a major producer (from its Canadian ores) of six platinum group metals — platinum, palladium, rhodium, ruthenium, iridium and osmium. The company also produces iron ore pellets and limited quantities of gold, silver, sulphur, selenium and tellurium. In addition, through its rolling mills division with plants in the United States and Great Britain, it produces wrought nickel, high nickel alloys and welding products; and since 1974, Inco has become a major producer of automotive battery products.

In 1975, Inco supplied 38.5% of the *Free World's* nickel consumption. Its major customer was the United States, which accounted for 41% of the company's metal sales in dollars, followed by Europe with 39%, and Canada with 11%. Inco supplied approximately two-thirds of U.S. nickel requirements. Although Inco has operating facilities in more than 20 countries, the bulk of its nickel is mined in Canada, and it appears that Canadian nickel deposits will continue to be an important element of the company's operations. The company is making substantial investments in developing nickel deposits in Indonesia and Guatemala, and is engaged in sea-bed exploration for nickel.

There appears to be an historical parallel between the emergence of Inco and Alcan as major Canadian based miltinational companies: both are of U.S. origin, the year 1902 being a critical one in their respective development, and the U.S. steel industry played a significant role in their establishment. The International Nickel Company was formed in 1902, through the merger of a number of firms in Canada and the United States, under the sponsorship of J.P. Morgan and Co. and the U.S. Steel Corporation. The head office was centred in New York, and seven of the 10 members of the first corporate board of directors came from major U.S. steel firms, as did the first president of the company.

In 1916, the International Nickel Company incorporated its Canadian subsidiary, the International Nickel Company of Canada, Ltd., and partly in response to Canadian government and public pressures to refine mine output locally, it built a refinery at Port Colborne, Ontario, which came on stream in 1918.

The year 1928 is a major landmark in the emergence of Inco as a Canadian based company. Through an exchange of shares, Inco (Canada) became the parent company, and Inco (U.S.) the subisidiary. It is interesting to note that on May 31, 1928, Aluminum Limited (Alcan) was incorporated in Canada to engage in the international aluminum business. However, in both instances, in 1928, while Inco and Alcan were legally incorporated in Canada, Inco's head office was based in New York, and Alcan's most senior personnel were resident in the United States.

Through a combination of acquisition, expansion and modernization, Inco, at the time of World War II, was the western world's largest wholly integrated nickel producing complex, from mining to refining and primary fabrication, with subsidiary operations located on two continents, and company personnel scattered in twelve countries. An interesting similarity between Alcan and Inco arose from the fact that these two companies looked to Canada for their raw material source — in the case of Alcan, it was cheap hydro-electric power, and for Inco it was the nickel ore body. To this day, approximately one-half of the corporate assets for both firms are located in Canada, and the bulk of their Canadian output is exported to sister subsidiaries and affiliated companies, largely in the United States and Europe.

Inco, unlike Alcan, however, has been more active in diversifying its activities away from the company's traditional metal base of operation. The first major step in Inco's diversification program was the acquisition in mid-1974 of ESB Incorporated, one of the world's leading battery companies. This U.S. company was a subsidiary of Inco-Canada's U.S. subsidiary, International Nickel Company, Inc. Sales of ESB Incorporated were $598 million U.S. in 1976, accounting for about 30% of worldwide corporate sales. ESB, in its own right, is a major U.S.-based multinational firm with 98 plants in 17 countries.

As a result of the ESB acquisition, the strategic importance of the U.S. market in terms of sales, assets and employees is now greater for Inco than Alcan; for example, sales — 50% vs. 21%; assets — 23% vs. 9%; and employees — 27% vs. 6%. In terms of ownership, the two companies exhibit similar characteristics; at year end (1976), "Canadian residents of record held 49% of the shares outstanding, United States residents of record 36%, and residents of record in other countries 15%."[20]

Unlike Alcan, however, Inco only recently (1972) moved its head-office organization from the United States (New York) to Canada (Toronto). It was in the late 1950s that the most senior executives of Alcan moved from the United States to their head office in Canada (Montreal). Inco, like Alcan, was recently judged by FIRA to be a "Canadian controlled firm"; but in the case of both firms, as of 1979, the chief executive officers have been citizens of the United States, although the boards of the two companies continue to be *Canadianized*.

Massey-Ferguson and Farm Machinery

Massey-Ferguson Limited (M-F), headquartered in Toronto, is one of Canada's oldest and largest multinational operations. As an international organization, it can trace its corporate thrust into the international business as far back as the 1880s. The predecessor of M-F was the Massey Harris Co. Limited, which merged with Harry Ferguson Limited in 1953 to form Massey-Harris-Ferguson, whose name was changed to Massey-Ferguson Ltd. in 1958. M-F is a holding company with over 100 subsidiaries and associates in which it holds minority interests; it manufactures in 18 countries, and sells farm machinery, industrial and construction machinery, and diesel engines through subsidiaries, associated and franchised distributors and dealers in more than 130 countries.

With a sales volume of $2.8 billion in 1976, corporate management contended that it was the largest manufacturer, in the western world, of agricultural tractors and sugar cane harvesters; that its aggregate sales in agricultural equipment were exceeded only by the sales of two U.S. multinational competitors; and that it manufactured more high-speed diesel engine units, worldwide, than any competing producer. M-F is not only one of the biggest firms in Canada, it also ranks as one of the world's largest manufacturers of agricultural equipment. This distinction is an important one to bear in mind when one compares the size of Canadian multinational corporations with those of the United States. The largest manufacturers in the United States tend to rank high among the largest worldwide, but the largest in Canada only rank high in the context of industry/product specific categories.

The growth of M-F since the mid-1960s has been triggered by an active program of acquisition, expansion and integration. Most of the acquisitions took place in the industrialized west; that is, United States, U.K., Italy and Germany. In 1976, M-F had a manufacturing base of some 50 plants, containing 25 million square feet situated in 12 countries. This is the core of the company's manufacturing system; in addition, through corporate arrangements with associate companies or licensees, M-F manufactured in 18 other countries.

M-F has pursued a program of corporate integration in all key areas of commercial activity; however, it is in production and sourcing that the company has gained considerable success and business acclaim. The corporate policy is designed to promote maximum interchangeability of component parts, especially for tractors and combines, in order to increase production efficiencies on a worldwide basis. In the company's 1975 annual report, management stated:

> Highly productive results have been secured from each major capital investment through the use of our worldwide production scheduling system and our logistics network of multinational sources. In addition, production costs continue to be kept under control by product integration

— switching from buy to make . . . through product design and manufacturing planning, emphasis continues to be placed upon interchangeability and commonality to obtain cost benefits and sourcing flexibility.[21]

M-F's strategy aims at sourcing complete machines for specific markets from those M-F plants which can supply them at the lowest cost. Flexibility, via interchangeability of component parts of the machine, is not simply realized by plant location, but also by phase of manufacturing, which takes place in the individual plant. Corporate integration is especially evident in the North American operations of M-F, because there are no tariffs on shipments of agricultural equipment between Canada and the United States. For this reason, a group of M-F operating subsidiaries conduct the company's business in this combined market, with some products manufactured in the United States and others in Canada.

In 1976, the relative corporate importance of Canada and the United States, measured in terms of sales, assets and employees, were as follows: 8% vs. 23% (sales); 11% vs. 26% (assets); and 12% vs. 9% (employees). Employing the same yardstick for the two country comparison (Canada vs. United States), the 1966 figures were as follows: 10% vs. 31% (sales); 18% vs. 16% (assets); and 17% vs. 11% (employees). In that 10 year interval, North America's share of the company's total sales dropped from 41% to 31%, while Latin America, Asia, Africa and Australia increased their relative sales importance. But in terms of assets, both globally and in the context of the company's North American operations, the picture is different: the United States now accounts for slightly more than one-quarter of total assets. The sales to assets ratio is approximately 1:1 and it appears that even though free trade exists between the United States and Canada, the company has opted to service the U.S. market largely from U.S. plants. While transportation costs may be a ready made explanation for establishing and acquiring U.S. plants, rising Canadian labour costs and the lower productivity of its Canadian plants, led M-F's Canadian management to invest more heavily in the United States in recent years.

M-F's entry into the U.S. market parallels the approach favoured by many of today's companies which invest in the United States; namely, the acquisition route. In 1910, M-F acquired an implement manufacturer located in Batavia, New York. On the other hand, M-F's rationale for first investing in the United States is somewhat atypical. E.P. Neufeld, in his study of M-F, notes:

When it did obtain its first manufacturing facilities in the United States it was, paradoxically, because of the fear of free trade and not because of any attempt to circumvent the tariff. This is how it happened. Potential competition from the United States threatened to change with the 1910 campaign for reciprocity, that is, for free trade between Canada and the

United States. Massey-Harris (M-F) seemed to fear that if the campaign were successful, its Canadian market would be threatened by a flood of imports from the United States. Such fears were not entirely ill-founded. To protect itself from such competition, Massey-Harris hurriedly established itself in the United States by buying into the Johnston Harvester Company . . .[22]

Among North American multinationals, M-F is a pioneer: by 1908, it realized approximately one-half of its corporate sales outside of Canada. This achievement took place without the benefit of significant sales to the U.S. market. This is no longer the case; sales in the United States are significant, accounting for about one-quarter of total corporate sales; and M-F's U.S. subsidiary, Massey-Ferguson Inc., placed high in sales on the list of the 100 largest foreign owned companies in the United States.

Seagram and Liquor

The Seagram Company Ltd., like M-F, is a holding company. It is headquartered in Montreal, and multinational in scope, with operating subsidiaries and affiliates in 23 countries. The company produces a complete line of whiskies, gins, rums, brandies, vodkas, other spirits and wines and markets its brands in over 130 countries. In addition, through its subsidiaries, the company is engaged in the exploration for, and development, production and sale of crude oil, natural gas and related products. A further similarity between Seagram and M-F is that, in addition to being one of Canada's largest firms with a 1976 sales volume of approximately $2 billion, Seagram is also the world's largest producer and marketer of distilled spirits and wines.

The history of the present day company dates back to 1928, when Samuel Bronfman and his brothers acquired the shares of Joseph E. Seagram and Sons Ltd. of Waterloo, Ontario. This Waterloo-based firm began its operation in 1857, and by 1928, was a highly respected firm. The 1928 purchase was combined with the Bronfman's owned and managed company, Distillers Corporation Ltd., to establish a new public company, Distillers Corporation Seagrams Ltd.

Bronfman's entry into the U.S. market took place some five years later (November 1933), when a distilling plant in Lawrenceburg, Indiana was purchased. Thus, the acquisition route was again employed by yet another Canadian multinational. Joseph E. Seagram and Sons Inc. was formed to operate the distillery, and has since become the parent company in the United States. Expansion in the U.S. market has continued rapidly ever since. In 1976, the U.S. market accounted for 68% of total company sales and Joseph E. Seagram and Sons Inc., incorporated in Indiana in 1933 and headquartered in New York, is now an operating and holding company in its own right. It controls, through stock ownership, all of the affiliated distillery operations and sales companies in the United States.

In 1975, the U.S. subsidiary of Seagram Company Ltd. of Canada had a sales volume of approximately $1.6 billion U.S., ranking third on the list of the 100 largest foreign owned companies in the United States. The relative commercial importance between the head office in Canada and its U.S. subsidiary head office can be whimsically contrasted from the following quote:

> The company's executive offices are located in a four-storey office building which the company owns at 1430 Peel Street, Montreal, Quebec, and Joseph E. Seagram's executive offices are located in a 38 storey office building which its owns at 375 Park Avenue, New York, New York.[23]

That this is the case is not surprising, since 68% of Seagram's sales are realized in the United States while only 6% is made in Canada. Nonetheless, Seagram's market share in each country is comparable — 20% in Canada and over 19% in the United States.

Since World War II, Seagram's has been actively expanding its overseas operations (non-North America), while in more recent years, it has been engaged in a significant diversification program away from its traditional business of distilled spirits and wines. With reference to its policy of growth through internationalization, the M-F strategy of interchangeability and flexibility appears to characterize the Seagram corporate strategy. Sam Bronfman, who, until his death was synonymous with Seagram, offered the following explanation for the emergence of his company as one of the world's leading multinationals:

> I have always considered it most important that our business between the countries in which we have interests should be on the basis of a "two way street." Let me explain. We ship our Canadian, American and Scotch whiskies to France and Italy, for example, and we ship our French and Italian products to Canada, the United States and Great Britain. This "two-way street" premise extends to all the countries where we have facilities. It is this policy which is the spine of our business. It brings and holds together our worldwide operations.[24]

Inasmuch as 94% of company sales is realized outside Canada, and only 10% of the company's assets are located in Canada, with the United States accounting for well over one-half of total corporate sales and assets, it is not surprising that a U.S. subsidiary of Joseph E. Seagram & Sons, Inc. handles international sales. Seagram Export Sales Co. Inc., established in New York, was formed and given responsibility for sales in over 100 countries.

In 1953, a major change in the company's activities was initiated. In that year, the Frankfort Oil Co. of Oklahoma was purchased. In the words of Sam Bronfman:

Foreseeing the requirements for energy in the 1950s and the 1960s, and the almost unbelievable demand of the 1970s, I was motivated in 1953 to cause Joseph Seagram & Sons, Inc. to begin investing in the petroleum industry — the energy business.[25]

Growth through diversification received its biggest boost in 1963, when Seagram acquired Texas Pacific Coal and Oil Co., now known as Texas Pacific Oil Company, Inc. (incorporated in Delaware). This company generated total revenues of $140 million in fiscal 1975, ranking it among the top five independent producers in the United States. This Dallas-headquartered firm did no refining or consumer marketing itself; instead, it concentrated exclusively on finding, developing and producing hydrocarbons. Its major preoccupation today is with expansion.

In 1975, exploration and development property was held in 20 states of the United States and in Alberta (by Seafort Petroleum). North American holdings, largely U.S., totalled 2.5 million net underdeveloped acres, while overseas acreage amounted to 8.1 million net acres. Spain, Dubai, the North Sea, Kenya and the Philippines are some of the areas in which the Seagram's subsidiary, alone or in partnership, is pursuing its exploration activities.

The management of Seagrams is committed to developing the company's oil and gas business. Business and political events since 1953 strengthened management's conviction that the need for and value of new reserves would continue to grow. This conviction involves further exploration in the United States, but Seagram also accepts the larger risks, both political and economic, that are involved in international exploration. Management believes that overseas is where the discoveries of world-ranking new reserves will probably be made, and that this will influence Seagram's investment in the future. Current investment and Seagram's corporate strategy for the future appears to be U.S. and non-Canadian oriented, albeit multinational in scope.

SUMMARY OBSERVATIONS

The corporate vignettes of Canada's four major multinationals indicate that, regardless of their historical roots, Canadian or U.S., their investment and involvement in the United States is substantial, increasing and critical to the success of their corporate strategies. Moreover, the performance of the Canadian part of the operation is affected by what happens in the United States. While the corporate relationship between the Canadian and U.S. entities within the Canadian multinational corporation are to varying degrees interdependent, they are also asymmetrical; as is the case between Canada and the United States, in terms of trade and capital. Thus, although the headquarters of each of the four corporations is based in Canada, the sensitivity of the corporate executive in Canada to what happens in the United States is very great.

In the context of the present politico-economic environment in Canada, it is worth noting that Alcan and Inco were originally of U.S. origin. For this reason, it is not difficult to imagine that these two firms might wish to transfer their headquarters again; this time back to the United States. The move would not be a difficult one to make. Similarly, Seagram and Massey-Ferguson might see the merit of moving their headquarters. Some would argue that such a move would be more *de jure* than *de facto*; and the most likely site would also be the United States.

The probability of the foregoing scenario materializing at this time is not great, but it cannot be ruled out. If the present poor investment climate in Canada continues to deteriorate because of political, as well as economic, circumstances, the current transfer of headquarters' organizations between provinces, for example, Quebec and Ontario, may in due time, be overshadowed by moves involving some of Canada's largest industrial enterprises with substantial operations in the United States, to the United States.

For example, by the late 1960s, the management of Dominion Bridge decided that the company was too heavily committed to the fabrication of structural steel and the vagaries of the Canadian capital goods market, and were concerned about the long-term deterioration of Canada's competitive labour position. A decision was taken to build up a cash reserve by selling off some Canadian plants and other assets, and to use these funds to move into the United States. A dozen enterprises were acquired and consolidated into Dominion Bridge's operations between 1970 and 1978. During 1977, the firm secured majority control of Amtel, a diversified U.S. manufacturing concern, making $60 million U.S. by liquidating unwanted divisions, while retaining its engineering, construction and manufacturing activities. Amtel contributed one-third of Dominion Bridge's profits and sales in 1978. Consequently, annual sales of Dominion Bridge increased from $168 million U.S. in 1970, to $1 billion U.S. in 1978, and profits from $4 million to $34 million.[26] The firm's chairman and chief executive officer, Kenneth Barclay, had stated that further acquisitions would be made "to finish up the 1970s in line with the plan set out a year ago."[27]

Currently, Dominion Bridge still retains "a token head office in Montreal, but its real powerhouse is in the small college town of Hanover in New Hampshire, where its top operating executives are based."[28]

NOTES

1. Statistics Canada, *Statistics Canada Daily,* 11 April 1979, p. 4; Statistics Canada, *System of National Accounts: Quarterly Estimates of the Canadian Balance of International Payments, Fourth Quarter, 1978,* (Ottawa, 1979), pp. 19, 21, 66.

2. Statistics Canada, *Canada's International Investment Position 1974,* (Ottawa, 1976), p. 58.

3. Statistics Canada, *Canada's International Investment Position 1968-1970,* (Ottawa, 1972), pp. 27, 31, 92; *Canada's International Investment Position 1974,* p. 54.

4. Statistics Canada, *Canada's International Investment Position 1926-1967,* (Ottawa, 1971), p. 169; *Canada's International Investment Position 1968-1970,* p. 92.

5. Statistics Canada, *Statistics Canada Daily,* 21 Dec. 1978, p. 5.

6. Statistics Canada, *System of National Accounts: Quarterly Estimates of the Canadian Balance of International Payments Fourth Quarter, 1978,* pp. 66-67.

7. The difference between the Canadian and U.S. calculations re: Canadian direct investment in the U.S. is due to the difference in the definition of what constitutes direct investment; a lower percentage of foreign equity ownership is employed in the case of U.S. data to indicate direct investment. The Canadian figure is taken from *Statistics Canada Daily,* (Cat. 11-001E), Apr. 11, 1979, p. 4. For the U.S. data, see Report to the Congress, *Foreign Direct Investment in the United States,* vol. 2 (Washington: U.S. Department of Commerce, April 1976).

8. *Ibid.*

9. *The Financial Post 500,* (Summer 1979), pp. 8-21.

10. R. Vernon, *Sovereignty at Bay,* (New York: Basic Books, 1971). p. 11.

11. "Reorganization," *The Compass,* (December 1967), p.3.

12. R. Vernon, *Sovereignty at Bay,* (New York: Basic Books, Inc., 1971), p. 119.

13. E.P. Neufeld, *A Global Corporation,* (Toronto: University of Toronto Press, 1969), p. 390.

14. The following details are based upon "Dominion Bridge Co. Ltd. v. The Queen", *Dominion Tax Cases,* (Toronto: CCH Canadian Ltd., 1975), p. 5150.

15. *Ibid.,* p. 5151.

16. *Ibid.,* p. 5154.

17. The following books provide a historical overview of the four Canadian multinational corporations: I.A. Litvak and C.J. Maule, *Alcan Aluminum Limited: A Corporate History,* prepared for the Royal Commission on Corporate Concentration, Government of Canada, 1977; Samuel Bronfman, *Little Acorns,* a personal history of Seagram Co., included in the Company's Annual Report of 1970; E.P. Neufeld, *A Global Corporation,* (Toronto: University of Toronto Press, 1969); O.W. Main, *The Canadian Nickel Industry,* (Toronto: University of Toronto Press), 1955.

18. Alcan Aluminum Ltd., *10-K Report, 1974.* p. 1.

19. I.A. Litvak and C.J. Maule, *Alcan Aluminum Ltd.* Royal Commission on Corporate Concentration; Study 13. Ottawa, 1977, p. 20.

20. See Inco, *10-K Report, 1976; Ibid.* p. 9.

21. Massey-Ferguson *Annual Report, 1975.*

22. *A Global Corporation,* 1969, p. 21.

23. Seagram Distillers, Item 3, "Properties". *10-K Report, 1975.*

24. Company Archives

25. Company Archives

26. Dominion Bridge, *Annual Report, 1978,* pp. 3-7.
27. "After Many Profitable Acquisitions, Dominion Bridge on the Hunt Again", *Globe and Mail,* 4 June, 1979, p. B11.
28. *Ibid.*

Chapter 3

Direct Investment in the U.S. by Small and Medium-Sized Canadian Firms

Canadian direct investment abroad in the United States is concentrated among a small number of large firms in the primary resource and resource-oriented manufacturing industries. Much of this investment has taken place during the past decade, largely motivated by the need to grow through geographic and product diversification. Foreign direct investment undertaken by small and medium-sized Canadian firms has risen primarily from the corporate drive to exploit U.S. market opportunities, which were made difficult by trade barriers, particularly the non-tariff variety. A further critical factor prompting such investment has been the need to establish local U.S. support facilities, in order to serve U.S. customers in a highly competitive and marketing-oriented environment.

There appears to be particular cause for concern when CDIA involves small and medium-sized Canadian owned firms in the secondary manufacturing sector, which is the focus of this chapter. The reasons for this concern are many; however, the following two are generally considered to be among the more important: first, the secondary manufacturing sector is currently experiencing problems so that any corporate expansion outside of Canada by firms based in this sector is viewed as a loss to the Canadian economy. Given Canada's natural resource endowment, it is often alleged that when corporate diversification is geographic and in the U.S., the nature of this investment tends to be horizontal at the manufacturing level, rather than vertical. The perceived impact is that it is detrimental to the Canadian economy in terms of the export of jobs and capital.

Second, the high level of U.S. investment in the Canadian manufacturing sector has prompted Canadian governments in recent years to develop policies and programmes aimed at encouraging the *start-up* of new Canadian entrepreneurial ventures, as well as to *dissuade* foreign investors from acquiring such enterprises (for example, FIRA). The latter policy may be partially blunted by horizontal investments undertaken by small and medium-sized Canadian firms in the U.S.; for if they are successful, the end result can be an *Americanization* of their corporate strategy and structure. The consequences of such actions may limit the immediate economic contribution to Canada by the companies in question.

During the summer of 1978, the authors conducted a survey designed to provided empirical data about the reasons small and medium-sized Canadian firms invest in the establishment of affiliate operations in the United States, about the corporate form of their investment, and about the impact of such investment on their corporate operations.

The group of firms examined consisted of 25 Canadian owned firms with one or more affiliate operations in the United States. Each of these firms exhibited three key characteristics: (1) they were located in the secondary manufacturing sector; (2) they were small or medium-sized operations; and (3) they were all deemed to be technologically-based firms.

A technologically-based firm is defined as a company which emphasizes research and development or which places major emphasis on exploiting new technical knowledge.[1]

Information about these firms and their U.S. affiliates was primarily obtained through personal interviews conducted in the field, supported with material obtained from Canadian and U.S. government agencies, associations and chambers. A questionnaire guide was used to direct the company interview. The companies requested that their names not be identified in the study for fear of being unfairly criticized for investing in the U.S. at a time of high unemployment in Canada. Data were also collected from a variety of secondary sources such as annual reports,

Table 1

CORPORATE SALES, ASSETS AND EMPLOYEES FOR THE YEAR ENDING 1977

Sales (In $ Millions)		Assets (In $ Millions)		Employees (In Hundreds)	
Less than 1	(2)	Less than 1	(4)	Less than 100	(4)
1 - 2.9	(2)	1 - 2.9	(3)	101 - 199	(3)
3 - 4.9	(1)	3 - 4.9	(2)	200 - 499	(9)
5 - 9.9	(3)	5 - 9.9	(5)	500 - 999	(4)
10 - 24.9	(7)	10 - 24.9	(8)	1,000 - 1,999	(3)
25 - 49.9	(8)	25 - 49.9	(1)	2,000 - 4,999	(2)
50 - 99.9	(0)	50 - 100.0	(0)	5,000 - 9,999	(0)
100+	(2)	100+	(2)	10,000+	(0)

trade directories, Moody's Industrial Manual, company submissions to Parliamentary Committees, and one Form 10-K Report.

THE COMPANIES

The geographic distribution of the head offices of the 25 secondary manufacturers was as follows: Ontario — 15; Quebec — 6; and the West — 4. Table 1 gives a breakdown of their sales, assets and employees.

In 1977, five firms had a sales volume of less than $5 million, which according to the interviewees, would designate them as small among secondary manufacturers. This appeared to be the cut-off point between small and medium-sized operations, at least as defined in sales terms. Eighteen firms had an annual sales volume between $5 million and $49.9 million; this was the medium-sized operation. Two firms had sales in excess of $100 million a year, and at first glance, might be termed large. Upon further examination, these firms were viewed as border line cases, exhibiting more of the characteristics of a medium-sized firm, than a large mature corporation. For example, the two firms were owner-managed, recent corporate entrants, and were not ranked among the 100 largest Canadian firms. In fact, one of the two firms was a steel producer and was one of the smallest enterprises in its industry. Firms that appeared large by Canadian standards were often small by international standards.

Many of the firms could be classified as successful technical entrepreneurial ventures, well on their way to implementing corporate structures which reflect characteristics of professionally managed corporations. A major feature of the companies studied was that they invested substantial monies on corporate research and development programs. In recent years, approximately one-half of the population studied received government grants in support of their research and development. Two of the 25 firms went so far as to allocate a small percentage of their budget for pure research, in addition to product and process development work. Table 2 provides the range of expenditure on research and development.

Table 2

CORPORATE EXPENDITURE ON RESEARCH AND DEVELOPMENT FOR THE YEAR ENDING 1977

(in $ Thousands)

Less than 100	(3)	1,000 - 1,999	(1)
100 - 249	(6)	2,000 - 4,999	(4)
250 - 499	(5)	5,000+	(0)
500 - 999	(6)		

Considering the sales realized by the companies, their research and development expenditure was impressive. In the case of some companies, their research and development activity was closely linked to the services they sold which included research and development done under contract for Canadian and foreign governments, and international agencies.

REASONS FOR INVESTING IN THE UNITED STATES

All 25 companies had affiliate operations in the United States. What was particularly significant was that the opening date of their operations took place during the past decade, none before 1967; for example, two between 1967 - 1970, nine during 1971 - 1974, two in 1975, three in 1976, two in 1977, six in 1978 and one slated to be opened in 1979. Thus, when interviewing the companies, the executives were in a relatively good position to explain their reasons for investing in the United States. Table 3 provides a frequency distribution of the reasons, and their relative importance at the time the decision was taken.

Market Considerations

Home markets are rarely saturated, except in a relative sense. In this context, it is argued that, when the cost of developing new business is greater in Canada than, say, in the United States, the Canadian company may contemplate investing in the U.S. The literature on foreign direct investment suggested that such a

> situation develops most commonly in a mature domestic corporation which has surplus funds and management capability for which it foresees only marginal opportunities [in Canada.][2]

The foregoing observation was made with reference to the operations of large mature corporations, based in the U.S., and further stated:

> If it (the firm) does not diversify, it must generally be content to grow no faster than the economy in general. But the reward system of American business makes it imperative to grow faster than that. Some such growth can come via introduction of new products from research or from licensing others' research. Acquisition of other companies offers additional potential. Foreign investment is a third way to grow, a way which is often cheaper, possibly more profitable, and always glamorous.[3]

The benefits from investing abroad included the following: promoted new growth from a low-market share position, which could be quickly achieved through the acquisition route; management and technical know-how from the parent company could be readily transferred via a few parent company employees who may have formed the nucleus of the new subsidiary management team; foreign markets could be better serviced by a local subsidiary which provided a complete line of services in support of the company's marketing programme; profitability was often higher in the foreign market; and by expanding the domestic company's operations beyond its national boundaries, management could take greater advantage of product and marketing innovations.

While these observations helped to explain the foreign investment motivation and strategies of large mature Canadian corporations with affiliates in the U.S., they did not characterize the operations of our sample of companies, nor did they explain their reasons for investing in the United States. In the first place, none were large and mature; second, only a few had surplus cash at their disposal; and, third, all were involved in the manufacture of very narrow product lines. The last feature distinguished the operations of small and medium-sized firms in Canada, and was critical to understanding their marketing motivation for investing in the United States.

Table 3, under the market classification, shows that the first five (a, b, c, d, and e) considerations were judged to be among the most important reasons for establishing a U.S. affiliate. This is not surprising, since similar findings would apply to large mature Canadian companies. In the case of the latter type of firms, however, their product range tended to be much broader, and more diversified.

The crux of the answer lies in the fact that the majority of the companies interviewed realized for themselves a particular niche in the Canadian market, through the design and development of a limited product line such as measurement sensors and computer control systems for the paper industry. In this product category, as was the case with many of the other corporate interviewees, the company occupied a dominant market position, and was not in competition with large firms. The drive for growth led this company to invest in replicating its strategy and operations in the U.S., although it readily acknowledged the existence of opportunities to diversify its product line in Canada; for example, in terms of other industry applications.

The unwillingness to diversify in Canada was attributed to a number of factors such as reticence to enter a new product-market, especially if there was probable competition from large firms, many of which were U.S. owned; the cost of building up a new product line in the area of manufacturing, sales and distribution; as well as general hesitation to engage in new business fields, especially if the corporate waters were uncharted. For these and other reasons, many of the companies elected to probe the U.S. export market as a means of increasing company sales.

The third (c) market consideration was often pivotal because it pushed a number of Canadian companies into setting up U.S. subsidiaries. For example, a Canadian manufacturer of automotive parts explained,

Table 3

REASONS FOR INVESTING IN THE U.S.
(Ranked in order of importance*)

Market Considerations	1	2	3	4
a. Maintain or increase market share in the U.S.	22	–	–	3
b. Faster sales growth in U.S. than in Canada	21	2	1	1
c. Difficult to reach U.S. market from Canada because of tariffs, transportation costs or nationalistic purchasing policies	16	4	3	2
d. Diversify product line/geographic market	18	2	1	4
e. Increase responsiveness to U.S. customer demands and improve servicing capability	12	10	2	1
f. Integrate forward/backward	1	1	0	23
g. Promote exports from parent Canadian firm through U.S. subsidiary	2	2	0	21
h. Secure U.S. sources of materials supply	2	2	3	18
i. To export from U.S. to third countries	4	1	2	18

U.S. Production Cost Factors				
a. Availability of advanced technology	3	1	1	20
b. Availability of natural resources	1	0	2	22
c. Availability of fuel	1	0	1	23
d. Availability of stable labour force	9	6	2	8
e. Availability of managerial talent	4	4	5	12

U.S. Politico-Economic Environment				
a. General political stability	3	5	5	12
b. Trade Unions' Attitudes	5	3	4	13
c. More favourable taxation policies	5	3	5	12
d. Relative freedom from regulatory constraints	5	3	2	15
e. Easier access to financing	5	2	5	13
f. Wage/Price policies	7	2	5	11
g. Federal government economic incentives	0	2	1	22
h. State government economic incentives	2	1	1	21
i. Buy American policies	7	3	1	14

Firm's Canadian Corporate Resources and Capabilities				
a. Possession of superior technology	21	4	0	0
b. Growth in experience in international business	17	6	2	0
c. Growth in corporate capacity to finance investment via retained earnings/borrowing/issue of new equity	4	9	9	3

Canadian Politico-Economic Environment				
a. General political climate	3	6	4	12
b. Quebec-Canada constitutional debate	3	4	3	15

c. Trade unions' attitudes	....	4	3	5	13
d. Taxation policies	....	4	3	7	11
e. Regulatory constraints	....	4	2	4	15
f. Access to financing	....	5	3	5	12
g. AIB controls	....	3	2	5	15
h. Federal government policies	....	5	3	3	14
i. Provincial government policies	....	3	2	1	19

*Rating Scale: 1 - very important; 2 - important; 3 - of minor importance; and 4 - unimportant.

The American people are very proud, and there is a great tendency on their part to identify an American factory as being inherently or automatically better than a foreign factory as a source of goods that they are going to buy. I think that is a very big factor. People in the United States, if they know you are going to supply them with goods from a Canadian factory, seem to feel that in some way those goods will be inferior.

Most interviewees stressed that a major objective for their U.S. subsidiary was to project to their American customers the image of a U.S. oriented company. For example, companies which had U.S. sales offices and warehouse facilities, but no U.S. plant, often maintained a direct tie-line between their U.S. office and their main plant in Canada. Thus, U.S. customers calling the U.S. sales office could be linked into the main Canadian plant and frequently were not aware of the fact that they were talking to someone outside the U.S. All catalogues, literature, and direct mail pieces sent to U.S. customers made no mention of the fact that the company was Canadian. Canadian corporate executives typically kept business cards for both the U.S. and Canadian companies.

The strategy of downplaying the Canadian image was not out of the ordinary. Commenting on this phenomenon, the president of a geophysical manufacturing firm contended that,

For those who feel that the Canadian lamp should not be hidden under a bushel basket of prairie wheat I say forget it. It is true that the U.S. and Canada are each other's biggest customers. It is true that the Production Sharing program makes it easier to bid on the U.S. Department of Defense Contracts. It is also true that the U.S. markets are becoming increasingly chauvinistic in their buying patterns. It is also true that labour and protectionist lobbies have never been louder. Leave the flag waving and image building to Canadian Government officials. We don't feel we're misrepresenting anything — like the door on the Volvo we just don't make a big thing of it.

As for the remaining four market considerations, (f, g, h, and i) only (i) could be deemed to be important, but not necessarily critical to the U.S. investment decision.

One interviewee established a U.S. domestic international sales corporation (DISC) to take advantage of preferential tax treatment. Three other interviewees ranked the (i) consideration as very important because they intended to use their U.S. manufacturing base to launch an export drive into Latin America. A key finding under the market heading was that few firms with U.S. subsidiary manufacturing operations saw the establishment of such facilities as a means of promoting Canadian exports to the U.S.

U.S. Production Cost Factors and the Politico-Economic Environment

The relative size and growth potential of the U.S. market was the major reason for investing in the United States — a view shared by most Canadian firms, regardless of size.[4] Our study did not contradict this contention; however, our findings suggested that the difference between the Canadian and U.S. politico-economic environments was also a critical consideration in many of the investment decisions. The environmental factors included the following: higher profit expectations in the U.S. because of lower relative political and economic risks; lower cost and greater availability of financing; lower relative production costs attributed to less labour unrest and increasingly more favourable labour costs; superior productivity growth related to lower labour costs and more aggressive management, arising from a stronger committment to the free enterprise system; and less governmental intervention which promotes greater investment security for business.

The cost of production factors including land, labour, material, capital and management seldom constituted the rationale for the U.S. investment decision. For example, all interviewees claimed that labour costs were from 15% to 40% lower in the U.S.; however, only a few were involved in labour intensive manufacturing activities, i.e. where labour costs represented a high proportion of the value of output.

The production cost comparisons were rarely judged to be the predominant reason for investing in the U.S. as opposed to investing in Canada. Certain executives remarked that the impact of inflationary forces, price stabilization activities of governments, wage agreements, or changes in taxation, tariff and foreign exchange rates could quickly nullify or aggravate differences in the relative costs of production.

If, however, the production costs included the cost of doing business in the U.S. (for example, exporting to versus manufacturing in the U.S.) then tariff and non-tariff barriers, ease of financing and related considerations would have to be included in the total cost calculation. In this instance, the combination of the two groupings — U.S. production cost factors and U.S. politico-economic environment — was considered to be of comparable importance to the market factors by a number of interviewees, the majority of whom were based in Quebec and the

West. All interviewees singled out the extremely nationalistic and provincial posture of their U.S. customers in terms of buying *American* from U.S. based companies, as well as the *red tape* problems encountered at U.S. border points when trying to clear Canadian manufactured products through customs.

Canadian Corporate Capabilities and the Politico-Economic Environment

A major finding highlighted by the interviewees was that the requisite product and process technologies produced and serviced by them were commonly available in the United States. Thus, Canadian firms wishing to compete in the U.S. believed that they must establish U.S. bases of operation, since competition would then focus on product differentiation, sales effort, and service differentiation. This could not be readily accomplished via exporting, especially if the Canadian firm was small, and did not have the resources and/or proprietary protection to merchandise a truly differentiated product. Moreover, a Canadian presence was necessary in the U.S. in order to generate confidence among U.S. customers; that is, the customers would see this as guaranteeing supplies and the associated support-service requirements.

Superior technology and international business experience, but not financial resources, were among the important corporate capabilities which led many of the interviewees to establish U.S. subsidiaries (see Table 3). This finding should not be surprising, since a major weakness of most small and medium-sized firms in Canada was a lack of capital.[5] Obviously, this limitation was not a sufficient condition to dissuade the companies from investing in the U.S. The form of financing employed by these firms will be examined in a later section.

The key point made by many of the interviewees was that their competitiveness in Canada, possibly their survival, hinged on achieving market success in the U.S. In brief, geographical diversification was regarded as the route to getting bigger in the confines of the small Canadian market; however, only a handful of firms exhibited financial strength, and viewed this corporate feature as one of the very important preconditions to going abroad.

Not one interviewee singled out the present Canadian politico-economic difficulties as the sole reason for investing in the United States. Nonetheless, all six Quebec based companies admitted that the domestic political climate played a key role in their U.S. investment decision, but only after due consideration was given to the probable marketing and manufacturing implications for their Canadian operations.

As for the other interviewees, the majority of whom were based in Ontario, the environmental considerations were examined in relative terms, *vis à vis* the United States. On the whole, the United States was regarded as the more attractive site for corporate investment.

One symptom of the current economic and political difficulties experienced in Canada is the decline in value of the Canadian dollar. The actual extent to which capital flows may or may not be influenced by the undervaluation or the overvaluation of the Canadian dollar is virtually unquantifiable. Opinion is divided on the extent to which the 1978 exchange rate realignments may have reduced the size of corporate capital outflows in the form of direct investment. While there may be some reduction, our findings indicated that corporate capital migrated for a host of other reasons, and that the current exchange rate fluctuations have a limited impact on the U.S. investment decisions of small and medium-sized Canadian firms.

The findings suggested that the reasons for investing in the U.S. were seldom emotional and non-marketing. The following two examples (disguised companies) helped to illustrate this fact by highlighting the key factors which motivated two of the interviewed companies, one in Quebec and the other in Ontario, to establish subsidiaries in the United States.

The decision to establish a Geldart Research office and laboratory in the Denver, Colorado area was made during 1976 for the following reasons:

(1) Denver is a major centre for mining and hydrocarbon exploration operations and offices are maintained in Denver by a large number of mining and oil companies.

(2) Activity in the energy exploration and development field for uranium, oil, gas, coal and geo-thermal energy is currently at a very thin level and a significant proportion of the United States national effort in these areas is managed from Denver bases.

(3) Denver is one of the largest centres for United States Federal Research funding outside of Washington.

(4) The Denver-Boulder area is an important centre for government research laboratories such as those of the United States Geological Survey and the National Center for Atmospheric Research. The area also contains numerous research and development facilities supported by the private sector.

(5) Geldart Research has the potential for greatly increasing its penetration of the United States markets through a United States facility. The lack of such a facility has been a significant inhibiting factor with Geldart's U.S. customers in the past.

(6) The established expertise of Geldart in the earth sciences, exploration technology and contract research and instrumentation for

remote sensing of the environment, are ideally matched with the opportunities available in the Denver region.

Geldart's initial move had been to establish a small geo-chemical laboratory and photogeological facility. Contract work had already commenced on these premises. Particular emphasis was being placed upon energy areas in the Denver laboratory, and expansion into contract research was also scheduled after the geo-chemical laboratory was fully established. As far as possible, it was planned to integrate the Denver and Toronto capababilities in a complementary fashion.

During the initial phases of growth of the Denver operation, some corporate investment would be required, but this would be reviewed continuously with a view to achieving a self-sustaining operation as soon as possible.

For the reasons given, Geldart's management considered the growth possibilities of the Denver facilities to be very substantial, and, with a view to ensuring that the company's investment was applied with full vigour, the President of Geldart-Canada intended to make Denver his personal base during the period of establishment.

The prospect of losing U.S. customers for product X to an expanding U.S. industry prompted Kartash Products Ltd. to build a new plant in South Carolina that would produce as much as its two Canadian plants combined. The South Carolina location was chosen because of its proximity to Kartash's customers for product X. The plant could cost as much as $15 million and employ 100 or more people.

The cost of manufacturing in Canada was not a factor in its decision, nor was the offer of capital inducements to locate in South Carolina. A U.S. production base was expected to lead to large savings in tariff and transportation costs of products sold to U.S. customers. Employment at the Canadian plants, which were operating at close to capacity at that time was not expected to be affected then or when the new plant came into production in 1979. The domestic and international markets for product X were expanding fast enough to accommodate output of all three company plant facilities.

Kartash traditionally held a large part of the U.S. market; however, because its U.S. competitors announced plans of their own to expand production, these actions could jeopardize Kartash's market share if it did not make a similar move in the United States. The two Canadian plants were well located to serve export markets other than the United States, and Kartash would make intensive efforts to expand its offshore sales.

Product Diversification

Growth through product diversification, on the other hand, which is a strategy pursued by many large mature Canadian companies, was seriously attempted by only two interviewees. To date, one of the two companies failed, and as for the other, it is too soon to tell. The company that failed, a manufacturer of geophysical instruments, had decided in 1970 to diversify its product line to include audio equipment. The company's audio division, whose operations were concentrated mainly in Buffalo, New York, incurred substantial losses between 1971 and 1976. A change of management and a major advertising program instituted early in 1974, resulted in a temporary increase in sales, only to be followed by a sharp reversal related largely to the economic recession in the United States.

The decision to divest the company of this division, made in 1975, culminated in its sale to a large U.S. corporation. The sale was closed on July 25, 1975. The benefits to the company of this divestiture were:

1. release from ongoing operating losses of the audio division, which in 1974 and 1975 alone amounted to $264,000.

2. release of the capital tied up in the inventory, machinery, plant and land related to the audio operation. The total capital recoverable was in the order of $500,000, of which approximately $200,000 was realized from the disposal of inventory and machinery. The remainder came from the ultimate sale of the land and buildings in Buffalo. Realized funds were applied to reduce bank borrowings, and consequently, the burden of interest charges.

3. improvement in working capital resulted from the sale of the fixed assets of the U.S. subsidiary.

4. concentration of management efforts on ongoing profitable operations.

Management completed the consolidation of the company's organization by directing its resources exclusively into those technical areas which were basically profitable. This process had not been without cost or pain, as the selling and winding up of a division inevitably involved losses, with the disposal of inventory and other assets, as well as in severance pay and similar non-recurring expenses. Management also concluded that manufacturing activities should be concentrated on scientific instrumentation and, in particular, on devices that could be produced in the company's modern plant in Ontario. The experience of the geophysical instrument manufacturer was an excellent example of why most interviewees argued against the strategy of growth through product diversification in Canada and the U.S.A.

THE U.S. SUBSIDIARY

Canadian companies which establish subsidiaries normally do so after having exported to the U.S. for a few years. The typical sequence is one of exporting first, usually through distributors in the United States, followed by setting up a sales subsidiary with or without warehouse facilities, which may lead to the establishment of a plant for local assembly and/or full production. At the outset, the U.S. plants may engage in the partial manufacture of the Canadian parent company's product line. The items produced are often few in number and are not always the most profitable. U.S. tariff and non-tariff barriers, transportation costs and U.S. customer service requirements are among the key factors which dictate the product mix to be manufactured.

All 25 companies had sales in the United States: in 10 cases, 50% or more of total corporate sales were realized in the U.S. and only five companies had U.S. sales which accounted for less than 10% of total sales

Table 4

GEOGRAPHIC DISTRIBUTION OF CORPORATE SALES, ASSETS AND EMPLOYEES FOR THE YEAR ENDING 1977 (IN PERCENTAGES)

Sales

Canada		United States		Other Countries	
90+	(2)	90+	(1)	90+	(-)
75-89	(4)	75-89	(3)	75-89	(-)
50-74	(6)	50-74	(6)	50-74	(4)
25-49	(6)	25-49	(2)	25-49	(2)
10-24	(6)	10-24	(8)	10-24	(4)
1-9	(0)	1-9	(5)	1-9	(9)
0	(1)	0	(0)	0	(6)

Assets

Canada		United States		Other Countries	
90+	(15)	90+	(1)	90+	(-)
75-89	(4)	75-89	(0)	75-89	(-)
50-74	(2)	50-74	(2)	50-74	(-)
25-49	(2)	25-49	(3)	25-49	(1)
10-24	(1)	10-24	(7)	10-24	(3)
1-9	(1)	1-9	(5)	1-9	(1)
0	(-)	0	(7)	0	(20)

Employees

Canada		United States		Other Countries	
90+	(10)	90+	(1)	90+	(0)
75-89	(8)	75-89	(0)	75-89	(0)
50-74	(4)	50-74	(0)	50-74	(0)
25-49	(2)	25-49	(6)	25-49	(3)
10-24	(-)	10-24	(7)	10-24	(2)
1-9	(1)	1-9	(4)	1-9	(1)
0	(-)	0	(7)	0	(19)

(see Table 4). Nineteen of the 25 companies were also marketing their product line outside North America, and for six of these firms, more than one-quarter of their total sales were generated offshore. Geographical diversification was obviously the road to corporate growth, and the U.S. market appeared to be the major target for this drive.

All 25 companies invested in some physical operating presence in the United States. Fifteen of the 25 companies had U.S. manufacturing plants, but only three of them had more than one plant. Of the remaining 10 companies, four were essentially sales subsidiaries which owned/ leased/rented warehouse facilities. The geographic breakdown of the assets and employees of the *Group of 25* bore witness to the foregoing finding. Eighteen of the companies had declared assets in the United States, but only in 13 cases could it be considered significant, that is, in excess of 10% of total corporate assets. As for employees, 14 of the companies employed 10% or more of total corporate personnel in the United States (see Table 4). The geographic location of the Canadian operations in the U.S. was widespread: six in New York state, three in the Carolinas, three in California, two each in Colorado, New Hampshire and Texas, and one each in Florida, Georgia, New Jersey, Ohio, Pennsylvania, Tennessee, Utah, Vermont, Washington and Puerto Rico.

Management Control

Twenty-four of the 25 companies had wholly-owned subsidiaries, and one of them also had a partially-owned subsidiary. This last company had a majority owned subsidiary in which key U.S. personnel had some equity participation. This finding should not be surprising, since the companies were in the small or medium-sized category and tended to be owner-managed. Management of such firms liked to maintain personal control over their operations,[6] and since their U.S. subsidiaries were relatively young, it was charged that it would not be smart business to go public in the U.S. with an untested and unknown company operation.

The concern with control was not only reflected in the ownership of the subsidiary, but also in its reporting relationship to the Canadian parent. Seventeen of the 25 Canadian companies designated a president for their U.S. subsidiaries, and of the remaining eight, there were four vice-presidents and four general managers. Thirteen of the 25 chief executive officers were American nationals, 10 were Canadians and two were British. With one exception, the U.S. chief executive officers reported directly to senior executives of the Canadian parent company on all important matters — strategic and tactical. Much of the reporting was done along functional lines, that is, manufacturing, marketing and finance.

The U.S. subsidiaries enjoyed little autonomy, and only four of the

25 Canadian companies maintained a formal management contract with their U.S. operations, covering such areas as research and development, and exporting. The formal approach was considered unnecessary, since all key management decisions were taken in the Canadian parent company. Furthermore, for reasons of taxation and finance, it was felt that the informal approach was more practical since it allowed for maximum flexibility to decide when, how much and for what activities the U.S. subsidiary should be charged.

The financial structure of the U.S. affiliates varied substantially from company to company. In terms of the mix of debt to equity, the ratios ranged largely from 2:1 to 10:1. There were also significant differences in the extent to which debt was local or imported. A key finding was that most companies preferred high-debt ratios and a minimum of equity capital for their U.S. subsidiaries, with much of the debt capital raised in the U.S.

The preference for this type of financing was not surprising, since many of the firms were privately held, and those that were public, were closely held by a few individuals. The preoccupation with control was a key reason the U.S. subsidiaries were thinly capitalized and thus highly leveraged. The relative ease of financing in the U.S. was the major reason for borrowing locally. The experience of all interviewees was that the U.S. unit banking system was more responsive to the financial needs of small and medium-sized firms, the collateral requirements were less exacting, and the interest rates were generally lower.

Finance

Fourteen of the 25 companies raised most of their capital requirements in the U.S., and of the remaining 11, six of the companies financed their U.S. operations wholly in Canada, through the use of corporate funds and debt capital obtained from Canadian financial institutions. The cost of establishing the U.S. subsidiary ranged anywhere from $50,000 to $15 million, but most of the operations fell significantly below the $1 million level.

The partial or complete acquisition of an existing U.S. operation, or the establishment of a new facility were generally the two ways of physically expanding into the U.S. Only three of the 25 companies studied employed the acquisition strategy, while many of the other companies set up their U.S. operations through a combination of lease/ rental arrangements. This approach was the dominant one because it was the least costly and risky. Moreover, it was also one of the few ways in which a Canadian company, financially strapped, could expand its operations into the U.S.

A few examples may help to illustrate how some of the U.S. manufacturing operations were organized with minimal company financing. A

Quebec based manufacturer of product M, for example, set up a manufacturing operation in New Hampshire by leasing a site and building, and by purchasing most of the required equipment and machinery from a bankrupt manufacturer. In addition, the Quebec firm was able to hire an excellent labour force, since the location of its plant was within easy driving distance of where the bankrupt firm had been located. Most of the former employees were still without jobs; they were non-unionized; their wages were 30% lower than in Quebec and their productivity was higher.

Companies whose subsidiaries were large sales affiliates tended to rent/lease their warehouse facilities. In some cases, they used their U.S. distributors' facilities as a proxy for their own, including secretarial services. However, they always made certain that the stationery, answering services and related activities were conducted as if a fully integrated Canadian/U.S. operation was in existence.

The U.S. Industrial Revenue Bond was considered to be an attractive way of financing the establishment of new plants. Three of the 25 companies took advantage of this option. Most, however, were unfamiliar with it, and some of them could have benefited from exploiting this financial instrument.

Industrial Revenue Bonds are securities issued by Industrial Development Authorities for the purpose of purchasing land, and constructing and equipping manufacturing and/or distribution facilities for lease to responsible companies. If a company selects a site for a factory in one of the states which has revenue bond financing, then it may benefit from the following advantages of revenue bond financing:

1. *Low Interest Rate* — since the interest is tax free to the bondholders, the company pays a lower interest on the bonds. Generally IRB interest rates are 2% below corporate bonds and mortgage financing.

2. *100% Financing of Land, Building, and Equipment* — development and financing costs of a project as well as the cost of land, buildings and equipment may be financed. Most conventional methods of financing, (that is, mortgage financing) require 30% or more of an equity position by the borrowing company. The costs that may be funded include: a) site selection, b) site preparation and site utilities, c) design, engineering and construction of manufacuturing or distribution building, d) purchase and installation of machinery and equipment; furnishing and equipping of office area, e) payment of fiscal, legal and printing expenses of Bond issuance, f) capitalization of interest charges during construction of the project and for a one-year period thereafter.

3. *Repayment Schedule Tailored to Lessee Company* — it may be level debt service or a variation of this. Generally the shorter the maturity

schedule, the lower the total interest cost. Principal payments may be delayed to give the company time to go through the necessary start-up and developmental stages before any substantial payment is made toward amortizing the indebtedness. A 20 year maturity is considered standard in this form of financing. Balloon or term maturities may also be used. Generally, the bonds are not callable for the first few years, except in the case of damage or destruction of the property or condemnation. Provisions for such events are written into the Lease Agreement, as is the price at which the bond issue may be redeemed after the expiration of the non-callable period.

4. *Project Fitted to Lessee Company's Needs* — the issuing authority has no control or authority over the construction nor in the ordinary operation of the project by the lessee. The lessee may make structural changes to the building and replace the machinery and equipment within certain limits. There is no restriction on replacement equipment to be purchased with corporate funds. Maintenance of the property and adequate insurance is the direct responsibility of the lessee.

5. *Company May Buy or Lease Project at End of Payment Schedule* — a company may continue to lease the facility at an annual rental or to purchase the facility for a nominal sum, if provided for in the lease agreement.

6. *Tax Advantages May Be Realized* — depending on the state and community, the company may be able to achieve reductions in taxes such as the property taxes.

The only significant disadvantage is the $5 million U.S. capital expenditure limit, as set forth by the United States Internal Revenue Code. For a six year period commencing three years prior to the date of delivery of the bonds, and ending three years after said delivery, total capital expenditures made by the corporation at, or in connection with the project, may not exceed $5 million, irrespective of the source of payment for, or funding of, any such capital expenditures. All capital expenditures for facilities of a depreciable nature made and principally used by the lessee company are taken into consideration in determining the $5 million limit. However, if the items installed at the project were purchased or acquired by the corporation more than three years prior to the date of the delivery of the bonds, they would not be chargeable against the $5 million limitation. When a violation occurs, the bonds' interest becomes taxable as of the date of the violation.

The conditions and flexibility of the Industrial Revenue Bond is especially attractive for Canadian firms with limited financial means. The Ontario automotive parts manufacturer, who recently opened up a new manufacturing plant in the U.S. South, pointed out that

. . . this form of financing will not conflict with restrictions on any out-standing corporate debt arrangements, and can be accomplished without disturbing the natural market for traditional corporate debt issued or to by issued by the company.

Another manufacturer, this one based in Alberta, offered the following remarks:

One thing that helps in the United States is that if you want to put a factory up, you can get a low-interest loan under a bonding arrangement from many of their municipalities. They have very competitive rates there. They seem to have very aggressive local business groups or development agencies, even in small towns. Our factory was built by the business community in a small mid-western town using these bonds, because they wanted us to go to that town.

Community involvement was apparent and real. In the case of the auto parts plant, at the time the ground breaking ceremonies took place, the participants included the mayor of the small town (a community of 45,000), an official of the Enterprise Development Division of the state, the president of the construction company, a former mayor of the community, a local judge, the president of the U.S. subsidiary, a mayor of a neighbouring town, and a minister of the First Baptist Church. Since the opening of the plant, the working relationship between the Canadian owned subsidiary and the local community had been excellent; in other words, mutually rewarding. In the opinion of the president of the Canadian company, Americans appeared to have greater respect for the contribution of the *free enterprise* system than did Canadians.

Manufacturing and Warehousing

Fifteen of the 25 companies had manufacturing plants in the U.S., and three had multiplant operations. The three included a steel producer, a mobile home manufacturer, and a telecommunications equipment manufacturer. The square footage of these plants ranged from a low of 4,000 to a high in excess of 200,000 with most concentrated around the 100,000 mark. The staff employed at these plants were as few as 10 in one instance, and as many as 800 in another. In only three cases were the U.S. subsidiary operations, in size and output, bigger than their Canadian parent.

These three companies included an Ontario based steel producer, a Quebec hardware manufacturer, and a British Columbia aircraft designer. The steel producer had one mini-steel mill in Canada, but two in the U.S. While the combined output in tonnage of the U.S. mills exceeded the Canadian total, the plant staff employed in both countries were comparable in size. In the case of the hardware manufacturer,

U.S. acquisitions and the concentration of their manufacturing activities in one new large plant have made the American operation bigger than the Canadian. However, as in the case of the steel producer, the size of the Canadian labour force exceeded that of the U.S. The difference may have been explained in terms of the relatively more modern U.S. plants, and the greater degree of specialization because fewer products were manufactured, and their production runs were significantly longer than in the Canadian parent operations.

The aircraft example was a special case. The company was incorporated in 1970 to build a prototype STOL aircraft. In 1971, management decided to produce the prototype in the state of Washington to qualify for FAA certification, and because aircraft expertise was readily available from Boeing in Seattle. Thus, the Seattle operations became significantly larger than the total equivalent Canadian base. The original idea was to do the manufacturing in Canada, once the prototype flew. In 1974, however, management decided that manufacturing should also take place in the U.S. because of a lack of Canadian government financing, and the higher costs of manufacturing in Canada.

The plane flew in 1975, but had yet to be certified. Management estimated that it required about $5 million to get into commercial operations, and was at the time trying to raise this money. The subsidiary in the U.S. had to qualify as a U.S. citizen in order to meet the standards for FAA certification. A cosmetic change was made to satisfy this requirement, while still making certain that the Canadian parent retained control of the operation. The gist of this requirement and its satisfactory resolution could be quickly gleaned from the following two paragraphs:

> Following the first flight it was noted that the Subsidiary did not qualify as a "United States Citizen." Under the pertinent United States statute, a United States citizen, as far as a corporation is concerned, is defined in effect as a corporation, incorporated under the laws of the United States or any State thereof, or which the President and at least two-thirds of the directors and other managing officers are United States citizens and of which are least 75% of the outstanding voting shares are owned or controlled by United States citizens.
>
> The matter was discussed at length with the regional counsel for the Federal Aviation Administration who advised that the aircraft could be transferred to and registered in the name of an individual United States Citizen and held by him on behalf of the Parent or it could remain registered in the name of the Subsidiary if the necessary action was taken to qualify the Subsidiary as a United States Citizen. The regional counsel further advised that it would be in order for an individual or corporate United States citizen to hold the aircraft in trust for and on behalf of the Parent and indicated that it was a common practice for aircraft manufacturers to have a subsidiary or a company of convenience so that new

aircraft on leaving the production line could be registered in its name pending sale and registration in the name of the ultimate purchaser.[7]

The question regarding incorporation in the U.S. was viewed as straight forward by the interviewees. Twenty-three of the 25 companies incorporated their subsidiaries as U.S. companies, while the remaining two registered them as branches of the Canadian firm. The major reason for the latter option was to offset the U.S. branch losses against the total profits on the Canadian operation. It was pointed out, however, that once profits were realized in the U.S., the branch status would be changed to a U.S. incorporated citizen.

Ten of the 25 companies were largely sales subsidiaries with warehouse facilities. The structure of this type of operation was simple. For example, an Ontario manufacturer of bicycles leased a 30,000 square foot warehouse in New Hampshire to stock his Canadian made products. An inventory of approximately one million dollars was maintained in the warehouse, and was used to help finance the company's U.S. operations. The Ontario firm held an option to lease or purchase 4½ acres of land adjacent to the warehouse facility. The present site could be converted into an assembly/manufacturing plant which was the direction management hoped to take in the future. At that time, all major U.S. orders were serviced by the company's two plants in Ontario and Quebec. The New Hampshire warehouse was limited to servicing repeat orders for a narrow line of bicycles, while maintaining spare parts for all Canadian products exported to the United States.

Five of the 10 companies were sales subsidiaries which subcontracted some of their distribution and warehousing activities to U.S. distributors. These distributors, however, functioned as an extension of the Canadian companies' operations in the U.S. The facade was used to make the U.S. customers believe that they were dealing with a U.S. based operation.

SUMMARY OBSERVATIONS

International business expertise was common to all the companies studied. The senior executives interviewed generally believed that in order to sustain their competitiveness in Canada, they had to achieve sales success in the United States. Partly in response to this concern and challenge, this group of small and medium-sized companies established U.S. subsidiary operations. While the motivation for such investment may be viewed as being part of a defensive marketing strategy, it is equally important to recognize that the formulation of this strategy was accelerated by deteriorating economic and political circumstances in Canada.

The establishment of the U.S. subsidiary normally took place after exporting for a few years to the U.S. market. Initially, most of the subsidiaries were sales and warehousing operations, leading to assembly, partial or full manufacturing organizations. Since the firms in question were generally small and recent U.S. corporate entrants, only a few had U.S. plants which manufactured in full their Canadian developed and designed products. Most, however, hoped that success in the U.S. would lead them in this direction, that is, the opening of a manufacturing plant.

The U.S. subsidiaries were tightly controlled by their Canadian parents, and all key decisions were made by executives in Canada, particularly those involving financial outlays. While the amount of capital invested outside Canada by this group of companies was not significant, two important observations can be made about such investment in terms of its impact on small business in Canada.

First, the financial resources of small and medium-sized firms are generally limited. Thus, if a company expands into the U.S., its financial ability to pursue similar investment opportunities in Canada will be constrained, because it will have had to mortgage most of its assets in support of its U.S. project. Raising the capital in the U.S. may reduce the impact of such investment on capital outflows, but it will hardly improve the financial capability of the Canadian firm to raise capital in Canada or elsewhere for other investment undertakings.

Second, the limited size of the Canadian market and the general reservation about growing through product diversification prompts small and medium-sized firms to consider investing in the United States. If such a decision leads to the establishment of a manufacturing plant in the U.S., the former Canadian/U.S. export business is normally transferred to the U.S. operation. The new gap in Canadian production can be filled through an increase of either Canadian or offshore sales. If this result is not forthcoming, the competitiveness of the Canadian firm can be jeopardized, particularly at a time when its resources are strained because of the competing demands emanating from its newly established U.S. subsidiary. A number of the firms interviewed closed their U.S. plant operations for this reason, and their experiences have not gone unnoticed.

The press tends to publicize outbursts by executives who threaten to move their Canadian manufacturing operations to the U.S. because of deteriorating politico-economic circumstances in Canada. Of the 25 companies studied, only two had either moved their head office or their manufacturing operations to the U.S. In the former case, the head office was moved because of estate tax considerations. In the latter case, the market was in the U.S. and since U.S. government standards determined the potential acceptability of the product, the Canadian firm found it expedient to design and test the prototype in the state of Washington and not in the province of British Columbia.

Is there any truth to the allegations regarding the exodus of Canadian firms to the U.S.? Our findings from this group of 25 firms suggested that there was no exodus. We encountered few companies which seriously contemplated moving their total operations to the U.S. The exceptions were essentially one-man operations, such as the Ontario assembler of packaging machines who employed some 12 people, leased his manufacturing space and machinery, and exported 80% of his yearly sales volume of about $600,000 to the United States. From his perspective, he had little to lose and much to gain by transferring his company site to Texas, and he offered the following reasons for wishing to make the move:

— Texas has no state corporation taxes
— Texas has no state personal taxes
— Texas industrial space rates are much lower
— U.S. labour rates are lower and productivity higher
— His major market is in the U.S.A.
— Financing is more readily available in the U.S. at interest rates below 8%
— Despite the alleged unemployment situation, good Canadian workers are almost unobtainable
— High cost of financing in Canada, especially with FBDB, and there is even a penalty on early repayment of a FBDB loan
— Excessive documentation of duty drawback in Canada
— Generally higher Canadian business and personal taxes
— Multiplicity of forms from all levels of government which have to be filled in Canada.

The possibility of more owner-managers of small firms contemplating moving their entrepreneurial talents to the U.S. should not be lightly dismissed. These individuals are easily affected by both economic and political developments. In the case of the latter, on the psychological level, which also impacts on a company's investment decision-making process, Canadian opinion makers are basically viewed as hostile towards business, especially when it is profitable; Canadian labour seems to resist changes that are designed to promote Canadian productivity; and government officials, both elected and appointed, appear to be less aggressive in seeking out and expediting business opportunities than their U.S. counterparts.

The lesson to be drawn from these perceptions is that Canadian public policy towards business needs strengthening, not merely in terms of financial rewards; it requires some farsighted thinking and action on how best to stimulate and recognize the value of private enterprise at a time when business perception of its own status and worth in Canadian society is at a low point.

NOTES

1. A.C. Cooper, "Incubator Organizations, Spin-Offs and Technical Entrepreneurship", *Proceedings of the Indiana Academy of the Social Sciences, 1969*, 3rd Series, Vol. 4, (April, 1970), p. 33.

2. United States Tariff Commission, *Implications of Multinational Firms for World Trade and Investment and for U.S. Trade and Labour*, (Washington: U.S. Government Printing Office, 1973), p. 119.

3. *Ibid.*, p. 120.

4. See Report to the Congress, *Foreign Direct Investment in the United States*, Volume 5: Appendix G, Chapter 7: Canada, (Washington: U.S. Department of Commerce, April, 1976), pp. G-210 to G-256.

5. See I.A. Litvak and C.J. Maule, "Government-Business Interface: the case of the small technology-based firm", *Canadian Public Administration*, Vol. 16, (Spring, 1973), pp. 97-109.

6. See I.A. Litvak and C.J. Maule, "Profiles of Technical Entrepreneurs", *The Business Quarterly*, Vol. 44, (Summer, 1974), pp. 40-49.

7. Company Documents

Chapter 4

The Implications for Canada of Canadian Direct Investment Abroad

The layoff of 2,500 employees by Inco, the world's largest metal producer, in December, 1977, as well as the nine month strike during 1978 and 1979, brought to the fore a smouldering issue that had implications for Canada's domestic and international policies, namely the impact on Canada of investment abroad by Canadian firms. For the past 20 years, Canadian nationalists have performed the remarkable feat of maintaining a focus on the issue of foreign investment in Canada, while at the same time keeping in the shadows two issues: first, foreign involvement in Canadian unions, and second, investment abroad by Canadian firms. Public policy has dutifully followed this lead, so that Canada now has a battery of ill-coordinated policies towards inward investment, ranging from the Foreign Investment Review Agency (FIRA), through guidelines for good corporate behaviour, to a section of the income tax act, which disallows, as a tax-deductible expense, advertising in non-Canadian-owned periodicals, but manages to treat Reader's Digest differently from Time Magazine. On the other hand, policies concerning foreign involvement in Canadian unions, and concerning CDIA, are in a rudimentary state of development; and if possible, policy-makers have preferred not to talk about CDIA, especially if it is noted that Canadians have invested in South Africa and Chile.

In this chapter, a survey of the existing literature is provided which highlights the microeconomic and macroeconomic effects of outward investment on capital exporting countries and where the benefits and costs may lie. Then the impact on Canada is considered by the use of three case examples: Northern Telecom, Inco, and Alcan, all of which have substantial investments in the United States, as well as in other countries. Finally, the findings are summarized and some implications for Canadian foreign and domestic economic policy are outlined.

PREVIOUS STUDIES

The impact of outward investment on capital exporting countries, although of recent concern in Canada, has been actively studied in the United States and the U.K., and to some extent in Japan and other European countries. Views on direct foreign investment (DFI) range from those who argue that both home and host country benefit from it, that both lose, that the home country gains and the host loses, and that the host gains and the home country loses. Gains and losses in economic terms are in dispute, so that when the political dimension is added, the net calculation of whether DFI serves the national interests of home and host country is even more difficult to assess. However, research to date suggests two things. First, there is general agreement on the check list of economic issues which require examination, even if an aggregate assessment of all items on the list, costs and benefits cannot be made. Second, there is sufficient variation between types of investment, and that assessment requires, with the present state of knowledge, a case by case approach.

A recent study of the impact of outward investment on the United States noted:

> Indeed, one of our principle findings is that foreign direct investment is an extremely heterogeneous phenomenon. With respect to jobs and market concentration, for example, major differences exist among and within manufacturing industries. Generalizing about effects of foreign direct investment thus must be treated with extreme care, as must calls for sweeping policy approaches."[1]

Studies on the impact of outward investment on capital exporting countries had been motivated by a variety of particular issues. In the case of the U.K., the concerns had centred around the balance of payments impact of outward investment, while for the Unites States, a main concern had been the employment impact stemming from union claims that outward investment had involved the export of jobs from the United States. The question of technology transfer had also been examined, as well as the overall contribution which outward investment made to the national income of the capital exporting country. Other isssues had included the impact on industrial structure and domestic competition, on monetary, fiscal and exchange rate policies, and on the access which countries obtained to an assured flow of natural resources. Political dimensions had also been included, such as the extent to which a country's foreign policy could be assisted or thwarted through the foreign operations of its companies.

The concerns of countries with less outward investment than the U.S. and U.K. are of interest to Canada. Japan, for example, uses outward investment to gain access to markets, raw materials and cheap foreign labour, because of the nature of the economy which depends on the foreign exchange earnings from its exports to purchase imported natural resources. Australia has likewise invested abroad to gain access to natural resources, while Swedish investment has tried to retain markets which were previously serviced through exports. A significant aspect of outward investment from small countries is that the domestic markets become of decreasing importance to the parent company, which may influence its future orientation and loyalty.[2] Major Swiss companies, such as Nestlé, find that the Swiss market accounts for less than 10% of total sales, but the strong affiliation to Switzerland remains. This may not be true for all such countries, unless there is close liaison and mutual respect between government and business.

In general, the impact of outward investment has been shown to be sensitive to the assumptions made about what would happen in the absence of the investment. Does it displace exports? Would a firm in the host country or another foreign firm have made the investment? These are some of the typical questions which have to be answered before the impact can be assessed, and as might be expected, their answers will depend on the circumstances surrounding each case. Thus, some of the more revealing analysis has emanated from the examination of case studies.

In the context of this chapter, it is not possible to review all the relevant studies. It is sufficient to say that the overall effect of outward investment on the capital exporting country appears to be benign in terms of employment, the balance of payments and the loss of technology, management and entrepreneurial talent. More importantly, these studies, mainly undertaken for the U.S. and U.K., have suggested how to approach an analysis of the issues.

The two major Canadian government sponsored reports on foreign investment in Canada had very little to say about CDIA. The Watkins Report in 1968 devoted seven (out of 427) pages to the topic, essentially describing the nature and extent of CDIA, as well as concluding that

> There is the economic benefit to the host country paralleling the economic benefit to Canada from foreign direct investment, a benefit that is potentially large for the less developed country.[3]

One interesting point raised was the fact "that in some industries there are important examples of direct investment abroad owned by Canadian citizens who are resident abroad."[4] The examples were not given.

The Gray Report in 1972 gave even less attention to CDIA, devoting about one-half a page (out of 523) to the topic in a discussion of the advisability of reviewing the activities of Canadian firms investing abroad. Some concern was expressed that this might lead to the movement of head offices from Canada.[5]

EMPLOYMENT

The debate over outward investment in the United States was precipitated by American union assertions that foreign activities of U.S.

multinational corporations (MNCs) tended to displace American jobs. For this reason, U.S. unions, particularly the AFL-CIO, have argued that the government should introduce protectionist policies; that is, both to limit the outflow of U.S. capital and technology, as well as to introduce and raise tariff and non-tariff barriers in the case of imports. The seriousness of this problem, as perceived by the American unions, was dramatized by their charge that approximately 900,000 jobs were lost in the U.S. between 1966 and 1971, most of them from the expansion of U.S. manufacturing activities abroad, and that the MNC was the vehicle for exporting U.S. jobs.[6]

Criticism and pressure from organized labour forced government and business in the U.S. to undertake and sponsor a number of studies to ascertain the accuracy of the union charges. These studies, however, did not limit their investigation to the employment impact of U.S. MNCs. Other impacts on the economy, such as the balance of payments, were included in the examination because of the interrelatedness of the issues. The U.S. Department of Commerce and Tariff Commission were the two major governmental organizations to tackle the foregoing issues, while the Chamber of Commerce and Business International did much the same on behalf of U.S. business.[7]

Using comparable if not identical data, the studies released between 1972 and 1976 contained documentary evidence which showed that U.S. MNCs in manufacturing, on balance, created jobs in the United States. In the case of one of the studies sponsored by the Department of Commerce, but directed by Professor Stobaugh of Harvard University, it was estimated that the employment impact of U.S. MNCs had been to create 600,000 jobs in the U.S., while the U.S. Tariff Commission had suggested that American FDI resulted in a net increase of 500,000 jobs. The studies may have differed about the number of jobs created, but their findings agreed on the point that U.S. outward investment had stimulated the domestic employment picture.

Differences in the estimated employment impact resulted largely from different methodologies employed, including the underlying assumptions and methods of calculation. Two limitations should be noted. First, the population of the firms which were surveyed included both multinational companies (operating in six or more countries) as well as national firms with some foreign direct investment. In each of the studies, the aggregate data used made no distinction between firms in terms of their varying degrees of multinationalization, re: production. Second, without exception, the focus was on U.S. multinationals involved in manufacturing. In this instance, however, one might have argued that, in terms of the characteristics of labour intensity, the findings of the studies would have tended to understate the employment benefits for the U.S. economy. This was in contrast to a sample which would have centred largely on the employment impact arising from overseas investment by U.S. multinationals in the extractive sector. The findings of the studies rested on secondary data drawn from the Bureau of Economic Analysis of the U.S. Department of Commerce, as well as on mail surveys and/or personal interviews, and case studies. Three employment effects were identified, with the first two receiving most of the attention.

Production Displacement

The key assumption made under this effect was that employment would have occurred in the U.S. had the production of the MNCs' foreign affiliates been carried out in the U.S. The domestic employment effect was measured in terms of exporting to foreign markets from the U.S., and importing output from the foreign affiliates back to the U.S.

The assumption underlying the production displacement effect was questioned in all the studies. This was done by surveying the MNCs to determine the corporate motives which prompted these firms to invest abroad. The key reasons identified included overcoming tariff and trade barriers, and initiating measures to prevent competitors from pre-empting a market. In other words, U.S. MNCs pursued *defensive strategies* and the corporate decisions taken did not choose between expanding production in the U.S. and producing abroad, but between continuing to supply an overseas market or dropping out. Thus, investing abroad was not pursued at the expense of domestic production and employment in the parent country. For this reason, the policy conclusion of the Department of Commerce was not to restrict the foreign operations of MNCs, since such a policy would not have generated a major expansion of domestic production and increased exports from the U.S. base of operation. The effect of such a policy would have probably resulted in a substantial loss of overseas markets for U.S. firms, accompanied by a significant expansion of the production capacities of their foreign competitors. As for importing production from the foreign affiliates back to the U.S., the studies indicated that the balance of intra-corporate trade was heavily in favour of the U.S. parent companies and not their foreign affiliates.

Export Stimulation

The contention underlying this effect was that a significant amount of U.S. domestic employment was generated through the production of American exports, which resulted from the establishment and expansion of overseas affiliate operations by U.S. MNCs. The Department of Commerce noted three reasons foreign investments stimulated U.S. export trade. First, a significant part of the overseas investment was made through an export of U.S. capital equipment, which usually required some continuous supply of replacement equipment. Second, many U.S. parent companies exported parts, components, and industrial raw materials to their foreign affiliates for further processing and assembly. This activity was especially significant in the automobile, chemical, machinery and rubber products industries where U.S. investment was quite dominant.

Third, an important volume of U.S. exports to foreign affiliates was resold without further processing and minimal assembly activity. The studies contended that sales organizations of U.S. affiliates were more effective than non-affiliated foreign distributors in merchandising U.S. made products in local markets. This tendency was attributable to the greater interest that foreign affiliates of U.S. MNCs had in promoting such sales, as a means of more easily rounding out their local product lines with those of their parent companies, as well as their mere presence stimulating interest in U.S. made products. Thus, the existence of local sales facilities, warehouses and trained personnel helped to facilitate not only the affiliates' produced goods but those of U.S. parents as well. For these reasons, the Department of Commerce study suggested that a considerable part of U.S. export trade could be attributed to the existence of the overseas affiliates of U.S. MNCs.

By internationalizing the location of production, U.S. MNCs were promoting intra-corporate trade on a global basis. This appeared to be borne out by two key trends identified by a U.S. Chamber of Commerce Task Force survey of 64 U.S. companies for the year 1970. One, the overseas affiliates found their parent companies to be a more important source of their imports than a customer for their exports; for example, in 1970, the foreign affiliates exported 27.7% of their output abroad to their parent companies, while purchasing 46.6% of their imports from their parents. Two, a substantial part of the international business transactions was conducted within the multinational corporate system. For the same year, 1970, 60.1% of the overseas affiliate export business and 72.8% of its import transactions were handled within the multinational corporate system, including the parent company in the U.S.

The U.S. Chamber of Commerce estimated that 25% of U.S. exports were usually shipped to the overseas subsidiaries of U.S. MNCs. This activity had a positive employment impact on home office administrative operations and supporting functions performed by other firms in the U.S. economy.

Home Office and Supporting Firm

The corporate infrastructure of the multinational parent company is usually expanded in terms of personnel with responsibility for directing and controlling the overseas affiliates, in addition to servicing many of its non-production requirements in such areas as research and development, marketing research and design engineering, procurement and sales, sales promotion and advertising, finance and personnel. Moreover, overseas operations provide job opportunities for Americans, although the job is performed abroad.

The major differences between the home office employment effect and the displacement and export stimuli effects is that, in the case of the latter two, the occupational coverage largely consists of semi-skilled and skilled occupational classes. However, in the case of the former, the jobs are primarily managerial, clerical and professional. Inasmuch as the U.S. is the parent country of most of the world's multinationals, the process of internationalization involving U.S. national firms has had a structural impact on the U.S. economy with reference to the skill and occupational mix of its labour force.

Employment in the U.S. has also been created for companies which service the operations of U.S. firms with overseas investments. The type of firms most often noted are those that engage in activities such as engineering, public relations, law, management consulting, finance and banking. Of the three effects, this is the least documented one.

TECHNOLOGY

Multinational corporations tend to dominate the development of technology in the United States; moreover, they are the key institutions through which U.S. technology is exported. U.S. unions contend that such technology transfers have undermined the U.S. competitive advantage in the global market place. It is charged that U.S. technology is combined with efficient, low cost U.S. foreign owned operations based on cheap labour, the output of which is then merchandised locally, exported back to the U.S., and to other countries, which, prior to the overseas investments, were serviced by exports originating from U.S. based production facilities.

It was noted in the discussion of employment effects that corporate motivation underlying the decision to invest abroad was largely defensive. For this reason, the assumption that foreign countries in which there are no U.S. owned affiliates would be serviced by U.S. exports was at best a tenuous one. Furthermore, the government and business sponsored studies indicated that U.S. exports of technology, far from contributing to the deterioration of the U.S. balance of payments, did in fact have a positive impact as indicated in the following findings.

While the high technology industries have in recent years been the major overseas corporate investors, the firms in these industries are the major generators of U.S. based exports, and are much less inclined to import in the same class of products. Between 1966-1970, U.S. MNCs had outpaced non-MNCs in the high technology industries as generators of net new exports, that is, new exports less new imports.

In addition to the net new export trade benefits arising from overseas corporate investment, the U.S. has benefited from inbound royalties and fees earned from the export of U.S. technology. Net inbound flows approximated $2.3 billion U.S. in 1971, and about 90% of this revenue resulted from the activities of MNCs. The importance of these earnings could not be underestimated either in the context of its contribution to the balance of payments, or its importance to the funding of research and development. In 1970, net inbound royalties and fees totalled approximately 11% of the $17.9 billion U.S. spent on research and development by all industries in the U.S. A further point to note was that U.S. exports of technology outweighed imports by a factor of more than 10 to one.

U.S. firms which have internationalized their production tend to operate in oligopolistic industries. Many of these firms view themselves as having a technological lead, that is superior technology, which is often the basis for their initial decision to locate abroad. A major reason for making such an investment is that the firm can then extend the useful life of its technology beyond the time when its exports, because of cost considerations, would no longer be competitive.

Not all benefits derived from the exportation of technology through direct foreign investment are export-related. There is strong evidence which indicates that the U.S. has benefited significantly from the international flow of technology, by obtaining the rights to foreign scientific inventions, innovations, as well as gaining access to an unquantifiable amount of technology, via the acquisition of foreign owned enterprises and the grant-back of improvements agreed to by foreign companies on licensed U.S. technology.

BALANCE OF PAYMENTS

One emphasis taken in the U.S. and U.K. government sponsored studies had been upon the determination of the recoupment period for the balance of payments of a given amount of outward investment. In addition, in the U.S. investigations, an estimate was made of the cumulative impact on the balance of payments after 20 years. The analysis of the recoupment period involved the making of a series of assumptions about where (region) the investment was made, the type of industry, the form of financing and what would have happened in the absence of the investment being made. The last assumption was the critical one in causing variations in the length of the recoupment period. For example, if the investment from the U.S. merely displaced exports that emanated from the U.S. and that would have continued, the investment made very little contribution to the U.S. balance of payments. If, however, the investment resulted in servicing a market which could not be serviced by U.S. exports, or which would otherwise have been serviced by another foreign firm, for example, Michelin instead of Firestone, then the contribution to the U.S. balance of payments was much greater.

Three sets of assumptions were used in the analysis for the U.S.:

(1) *Classical Assumption* — $1 of increased investment in the host country led to $1 of decreased investment in the investing country.

(2) *Anticlassical Assumption* — $1 of increased investment in the host country led to no decline in investment in the investing country.

(3) *Reverse Classical Assumption* — $1 of investment in the host country made no net addition to investment in the host country (it would have happened anyway) and led to no decline in investment in the investing country.

Only in the case of the Reverse Classical Assumption is there a positive recoupment period ranging between six and 10 years, depending on the region in which the investment is made. The U.K. study used a variation of the Reverse Classical Assumption and came up with a slightly longer recoupment period.

Critics of the U.S. studies have shown that the recoupment period could be shortened drastically by modifying the conditions relating to the Reverse Classical Assumptions. These modifications involved showing that (1) machinery exports from the U.S. were much larger than assumed in the case of new outward investment, (2) component exports from the U.S. were larger than assumed, (3) in many cases, because of host country restrictions, U.S. exports were not an alternative and thus there was much less U.S. export displacement, (4) where retained earnings in a foreign subsidiary were used in new investment, there was no outflow from the U.S., but there was a return flow to the U.S. as a result of earnings generated by the reinvested retained earnings, which accrued to owners in the U.S., and (5) failure to engage in further outward investment beyond depreciation may have undermined the earnings potential of existing outward investment. By incorporating these assumptions in the U.S. study, the recoupment period was shortened to one to two years for many regions. In the case of Canada, it was noted that the recoupment period was about one year, because the outflow of investment was immediately offset by one item alone, the purchases of machinery and equipment in the U.S.

The impact on the balance of payments varies with the region in which the investment is made, mainly because of differences in the degree of industrialization of the countries involved. In the case of developed countries, the opportunities for exports of capital equipment and components are much less than in the case of developing countries, where local sourcing is less feasible. For this reason, the recoupment period tends to be longer for investments made in other developed countries.

Balance of payments impact also varies by industry sectors. In primary industries, where the objective is to gain access to raw materials, the outward investment results in increasing home country imports of the raw materials, which will be much greater than the imports from investment in manufacturing, where the objective is to service one or more foreign markets. Overseas investment in manufacturing gives rise to imports to the capital exporting (home) country, similar to investment in primary industries, where the overseas investment is used to produce goods for sale in the home country. This situation gave rise to concern on the part of U.S. labour, that is, that U.S. firms were investing in Taiwan to produce television sets for sale in the U.S. at the expense of jobs in the U.S. It was noted in the studies that there were examples of this type of situation in the case of both Japanese and Australian overseas investment.

A differential impact on the balance of payments will also occur with the type of financing undertaken. Where the outward investment is financed largely from sources outside the home country, using either retained earnings, other sources in the host country, or some third country sources, there will be little initial outflow affecting the home country's balance of payments. At the same time, there will be little inflow of earnings on the equity invested by the home country, so that the recoupment period will be more dependent on the impact on exports and imports. Both the debt/equity ratio in the capitalization of the outward investment, and the source of debt and equity, will affect the recoupment period. A high proportion of debt to equity, with the debt financing raised outside the home country, may mean that the home country will not receive much in the way of earnings on the investment for some time, that is, it will lengthen the recoupment period, and may even have to provide financial assistance (balance of payments outflow), if the outward investment is unprofitable and default on debt financing occurs.

The studies also showed that the profitablity, and thus the home country earnings potential, varied with the way in which the outward investment was made. Takeovers or the acquisition of existing assets gave rise to higher earnings sooner than investment in a completely new (greenfield) enterprise. Especially profitable were takeovers of companies in developing countries, where the new management took over an existing company and probably injected superior managerial talent. In general, the higher the profitability of the enterprise, the more beneficial would the results be to the home country's balance of payments.

The technology content of the outward investment is also a critical ingredient for two reasons. First, there need be no financial outflow for the home country's balance of payments associated with the technology transfer, but at the same time, the technology can be capitalized in the overseas subsidiary and give rise to royalties and fees payable to the home country for use of the technology. Second, by having a variety of forms of payment to make, the subsidiary is able to remit a larger amount of earnings to its parent company. Similarly, if the parent company makes loans to the subsidiary, as well as investing in equity and transferring technology, its feasibility to transfer funds to the home country is increased.

OTHER ECONOMIC IMPACTS

The two economic issues emphasized in the surveyed studies were the impact of outward investment on the home country's balance of payments, and on employment in the home country. A variety of other economic impacts were touched on in the studies and will be commented on in this section.

The Reddaway Report provided the most comprehensive analysis of the effect of outward investment on a home country's (U.K.) national income. Contribution to national income arose from the return on the outward investment as a result of the profits earned by the overseas subsidiary, and through the effects which an additional subsidiary had on the productivity of the corporate group of which it was a member. The latter issue involved an attempt to measure the effects of knowledge sharing (for research and development and general know-how) in terms of the additional net benefits which arose, both from making the same research available for use in an overseas subsidiary as well as the U.K., plus the net benefits to the U.K. parent of research performed in the subsidiary. For example, it was found that U.S. subsidiaries in Germany performed research that benefited the parent company, and, in the U.S., general know-how was found to be beneficial to the parent. In the case of invesment in developing countries, no such benefits flowed from the subsidiaries, but the parent companies, and consequently the U.K. economy, did benefit from spreading its research over a wider range of output.

The analysis of the impact of outward investment on national income was the one place in which an attempt was made to adjust the financial statements of companies for the effects of inflation. Attention was given to adjusting for the historical cost of assets, depreciation and inventory costs. The annual return to the U.K. national income of an additional outward investment in manufacturing of £100 was estimated at 6% per annum compared to an estimated opportunity cost of 3% per annum, mainly due to the cost of financing the country's increased international obligations arising from the investment being made. In sum, outward investment was found to be beneficial as far as the U.K. national income was concerned. What should be noted is that the figure of 6% disguised a wide range of percentage contributions. For example, outward investment in developing countries was much more profitable than investment in developed countries; profitability increased with the length of time an investment was in place; and profitability was much higher where the investment was associated with a takeover rather than where it involved the establishment of a new subsidiary.

The significant economic impact raised by the Houston-Dunning study was the effect which outward investment had on the industrial structure of the U.K. Concern was expressed that the act of outward investment could be harmful not only in terms of investment being made abroad at a time when investment was needed in the U.K., but also because of the probable loss of intellectual capital. That is to say, at a time of lagging economic growth in the U.K., the need was not only for capital, but for the managerial and entrepreneurial talent to operate it effectively. The act of outward investment could well have been a drain of those resources, namely intellectual capital, which were really in limited supply, and once these resources had moved out they may not have easily been repatriated. In particular, the more attractive investment climate in continental Europe might have left a long run scar on the U.K. economy.

At the same time, it was noted that those companies which had a long history of outward investment tended to be the better performers compared to those firms which had elected to concentrate on servicing the U.K. market. The point is that superior corporate performance would benefit the U.K. economy, providing it was not later associated with the emphasis of the company's activities moving away from its home basis, to the point where research and development and other corporate functions moved away from the home country.

The Japanese version of the relationship of outward investment to Japan's industrial (manufacturing) structure was somewhat different. The Japanese government/industry coalition had cooperated to move abroad those industries in which Japan was losing its comparative advantage. Investment had been undertaken in the low wage economies of South-East Asia so as to transfer a declining activity from Japan and to make room for an activity in which Japan had a greater comparative advantage, and as a means of being able to continue servicing traditional export markets, both those in which the investment took place, and third-country markets. In some instances, Japanese markets had been serviced by imports from Japanese investments in South-East Asia.[8]

A major difference between the U.K. and Japanese approach was that, in the case of the U.K., outward investment had been controlled for balance of payments reasons, and more recently, there has been concern that such investment would weaken the country's industrial structure. While in the case of Japan, outward investment had been viewed by both government and industry as a way of keeping export markets, and of keeping Japanese industry competitive and efficient.

Neither individually nor collectively are the studies surveyed comprehensive in their assessment of the economic impacts of outward investment. Other issues which require examination are the effects of outward investment on inflation, on industrial concentration in the home country, on taxation, on access to raw materials and energy, on income distribution, on a country's position with respect to both trade policy and policy towards inward investment, and on the ease of implementing monetary, fiscal and commercial policy. This last point received some attention in the Reddaway Report, where it was shown that there was neither a positive nor a negative relationship between an industry's export performance and the level of outward investment in that industry. Thus, industries with good export performance had both low and high levels of outward investment as did poor export performers.

POLITICAL IMPACTS

The Senate Subcommittee on Multinational Corporations has promoted the political dimension of the public debate concerning the impact of the overseas activities of U.S. MNCs on American society. The public debate, initially triggered by the revelations about the International Telephone and Telegraph Company's activities in Chile, has since been expanded to include the general theme of corporate ethics with reference to improper payments and political graft involving U.S. MNCs abroad as well as in the U.S. Numerous hearings have been conducted by the Subcommittee, and while no specific policy recommendations have as yet been proposed, three of the key political questions raised by the Subcommittee, are worth noting:

1. Do the activities of the multinational corporations advance the interests of the people of the United States taken as a whole?

2. To what extent have our foreign aid programs been used to service the special needs of American owned corporations abroad and to what extent should they be?

3. To what extent is there a coincidence of interest between the multinational corporations and U.S. foreign policy in selected areas of the world?[9]

The internationalization of U.S. domestic enterprises is but one of the key developments that contributed to the closer linking of national economies. International transportation and communication have played equally important roles in stimulating the emergence of the multinational firm, thereby forcing national policymakers to become more sensitized to the political issues which arise from increasing economic interdependencies.

There are numerous case situations which show how the United

States government has been able to use U.S. based MNCs to serve the national interest. The most documented examples relate to the balance of payments guidelines and freedom to export restrictions. In each category, Canada, as the host country, is often the prime example of the politically injured or compromised party. There can be little denying that U.S. corporate expansion in the 1950s and 1960s provided some support for America's political and military position. Export restrictions, as applied through the Trading With the Enemy Act in the case of China and Cuba are but two examples which support the foregoing contention.

The importance of corporate growth and expansion has important implications for American foreign policy. The multinationals are among the largest and most powerful concentrations of economic power in the United States. That they seek to use this power to influence American foreign policy in directions which benefit them is also without doubt. However, it is equally true that American foreign policy has frequently run counter to corporate interests. While there is no simple statement of the relations, general corporate interest and the national interest have coincided. Corporate and political ethics have shared the American vision of a liberal world economic order.

RELEVANCE TO CANADA

Historically, the development of the Canadian economy has emphasized the exploitation of natural resources and more recently, the expansion of the service sector. The manufacturing sector has evolved with the aid of tariff protection, which has led to a high level of foreign ownership in many industries. The result has been the development of industry structures which are inefficient in the sense that they are high cost, and not competitive internationally. The export orientation of the economy has been associated with the sale of raw materials, and some of the largest Canadian firms have been resource oriented.

In other studies, it had been noted that it was the larger firms that had been the principal foreign investors, so that in the Canadian case, outward investment was likely to emanate from resource based firms which either invested in primary resources, or attempted to integrate forward into foreign markets in order to ensure a market for their raw materials. This has been the case with some of Canada's largest multinational enterprises. In addition, some of these firms have invested abroad, vertically backwards into natural resources. Consequently, if outward investment is associated with large Canadian firms, much of it will be resource related. To the extent that this requires the installation of heavy machinery and equipment, Canada is unlikely to benefit greatly from such exports or related employment, because of the limited size of this industry in Canada. At the same time, resource investments are unlikely to give rise to increased Canadian imports of raw materials, because of the country's resource endowment.

In the case of the Canadian manufacturing sector, a peculiarity arising from foreign ownership is the fact that about 20% of Canadian outward investment has actually been made by firms which are foreign (mainly U.S.) controlled in Canada. Opportunities for exports of Canadian capital equipment is likely to be limited, both for the reasons associated with resource investments, and because suppliers favoured by the U.S. parent companies are likely to be used. The earnings of these manufacturing subsidiaries may benefit the Canadian balance of payments at the first stage, but will involve an outflow of foreign exchange from Canada, if passed on to the ultimate parent company in the U.S. The form in which the outward investment from Canada is made is critical. If equity investment from Canada is highly levered with debt financing abroad, there is a high risk element with substantial opportunities for both gains and losses for the Canadian balance of payments.

A successful outward investment by a Canadian firm can have a significant impact on the future orientation of the company, especially if the foreign investment accounts for a substantial and increasing portion of its overall earnings. As the non-Canadian share of the company's business increases and becomes the dominant part of the business, then the orientation of the company will become less Canadian and more U.S., if this is where its principal market lies. As a result, future overseas investments may be made from its U.S. base of operations, and the Canadian balance of payments may be affected only in the sense that it does not experience the outflows and inflows associated with overseas investment. Ultimately, a company may move part of its headquarters from Canada to the U.S., and the balance of payments will be affected by the extent to which equity investments remain in Canadian hands and receive dividends from the company. This type of analysis results from two factors; first, the size of the Canadian market limits the growth of Canadian firms in Canada. Even if there were no foreign tariffs encouraging Canadian firms to invest abroad, transportation costs would still be a factor in Canadian firms investing abroad in order to obtain access to larger markets; and second, the investment climate in Canada may stimulate firms both to invest abroad, and to use their foreign subsidiaries as parents for further overseas investments. The case of Swiss multinationals provides some similarities in that the home market accounts for a small percentage of total sales and earnings. However, many of these firms have remained Swiss oriented.

The analysis of the balance of payments effects of outward investment has implications for the employment opportunities in Canada for different occupational groups. A positive benefit would arise in terms of an increased demand for clerical, managerial and professional personnel, provided that the expansion of the corporate infrastructure at headquarters is not shifted out of Canada. On an international scale, Canadian industry does not undertake a great deal of research and development, so that the benefits accruing to Canada from the overseas use of Canadian research and development is unlikely to be significant. Moreover, where research and development is performed in foreign owned subsidiaries in Canada, it is often for the purpose of adapting U.S. technology to Canadian conditions, and this may be of little value, if used at all, in outward investment. The programme of government agencies, such as CIDA, to promote outward investment in developing countries, could be of value to Canada if the profitability of such investment is as great as it was found to be in the U.K. studies. An offsetting factor would be the increasing taxation in some developing countries being levied on the earnings of foreign investors, which would limit the profits accruing to the Canadian economy.

The proximity of the U.S. to Canada, and the attractiveness of the investment climate in the U.S., can be expected to lead to further outward investment from Canada, which in turn may remove certain needed managerial and entrepreneurial skills. The weakening of the industrial structure noted in the case of the U.K., is something which could also take place in Canada with the removal of these skills. This appears to be taking place with the increasing expansion of Canadian direct investment in the U.S.

An evaluation of these issues within a Canadian context requires that attention be paid to the peculiarities of the Canadian industrial landscape, which have been noted, that is, small size of the Canadian market, the prevalence of foreign ownership within Canada, concern with inward foreign investment, and the form that the financing undertakes.

CASE EXAMPLES

In this section, an examination will be made of three Canadian firms, Northern Telecom Ltd., Inco and Alcan, in order to indicate how an evaluation might be made of the impact on Canada of their outward investment.

Northern Telecom Ltd.

Northern Telecom Ltd. (NTL) is a Canadian company owned 69% by Bell Canada, with the remainder of the shares publicly held.[10] The company manufactures and distributes telecommunications equipment, with sales made to Bell Canada, as well as to other telephone companies in Canada and abroad, especially to the United States. As indicated in Table 6 (Chapter 2), in 1976, NTL had sales of $1.1 billion U.S., assets of about $700 million, and 25,000 employees. The percentage distribution of domestic and foreign sales, assets and employees was as follows during 1976:

	Sales	Assets	Employees
	-----------------------% -------------------------		
Canada	86	80	80
United States	9	15	12
Other	5	5	8

From these data it could be seen that NTL's principal foreign manufacturing plants were located in the U.S.: additional plants were situated in Ireland, Turkey, Brazil and Malaysia.

The internationalization of NTL took place after 1956, at which time Western Electric in the U.S., a part owner with Bell Canada of NTL (then Northern Electric Co. Ltd.), entered into a consent decree in the United States. The effect of the consent decree was that Western Electric became the supplier of telecommunications equipment solely to AT&T in the United States; it sold its shares in NTL to Bell Canada and withdrew over time from supplying either products or technology to NTL.

The impact on NTL was considerable, forcing it to develop from scratch its own research and development capacity, and to become the manufacturing arm of Bell Canada, independent of the previous liaison which it had had with Western Electric and AT&T. In the initial years after 1956, NTL, with the assistance of Bell Canada, concentrated on developing an R&D capability. The end product of this effort is Bell-Northern Research Ltd., owned 70% by NTL and 30% by Bell Canada, which has established an international reputation in the field of telecommunications, and is the largest R&D operation in the private sector in Canada.[11] In a recent report, the Science Council of Canada stated,

> In secondary manufacturing Canadians have shown that they are capable of developing advanced technology when they want to. There is evidence, for instance, of continuing strength in the wire and cable sector of the electronics industry, and there are promising Canadian developments in optical fibre technology.
>
> A further outstanding example is Northern Telecom/Bell Northern Research. Here is a company which picked up the challenge of developing its own technological base when the flow of technology from the U.S. based Western Electric Company was curtailed by the American antitrust decree of 1956. Northern Telecom has now become a world scale Canadian firm in its own right.
>
> There is much to learn from this example and much to emulate if we are to build a strong industry and economy. Canada must use indigenous markets to build companies which can grow to world stature, and forge industrial linkages which will result in strong industrial complexes.[12]

A second part of NTL's independence strategy was marketing

oriented, to develop markets apart from Bell Canada both in Canada and abroad. Foreign markets could be captured either through exports or through production abroad. Given tariffs and the native-son purchasing policies for telecommunications equipment in many markets, production abroad was often the only feasible alternative. The U.S. market was especially attractive to NTL because of the general compatability of equipment throughout North America, the geographic and cultural proximity of the market and its size. Although Western Electric had 80% of the market tied to AT&T, there were opportunities for sales of equipment in the 20% non-AT&T market, and as Canadians are well aware, 20% of the U.S. market is about twice the size of the Canadian market. As a result, NTL's foreign operations have tended to be concentrated in the U.S., and it is the impact on Canada of these operations that will be discussed.

In the U.S. during 1976, NTL had 12 plants, sales of $100 million, assets of $105 million and about 3,000 employees. Six of the plants (in California, Kentucky, New York, Texas and two in Florida) were concerned with the repair and overhaul of telephone sets; one in Illinois produced outside plant equipment; two, in North Carolina and California, produced switching equipment; one in Tennessee produced telephone sets; one in Florida produced printed circuit boards and telephone set components; and one in New Hampshire produced voice frequency and test equipment. There were no plants producing wire and cable in the United States. In addition, an R&D operation, a subsidiary of Bell-Northern Research, was located in California.

Clearly the telecommunications industry is made up of a number of different products which are separate but related. Thus, these subsidiaries differ in degree of technological sophistication descending from switching equipment, transmission equipment, to subscriber equipment, wire and cable and repair and overhaul. The impact on Canada of NTL owning each of these activities in the U.S. may also differ.

In the first place, the six repair and overhaul plants are situated across the U.S. in such a way that service can be supplied to customers which have purchased NTL produced equipment, regardless of where it is produced. The expectation of customers is that an equipment manufacturer will service his equipment, and thus the establishment of these plants in Canada to service customers in the U.S. is not a realistic alternative. The only possible alternative is to licence or contract with a firm in the U.S. to provide the repair and overhaul service in the U.S., in which case, the jobs would still not occur in Canada, and the balance of payments impact would not be dissimilar to the present situation. The main difference between the present situation and this alternative is that NTL owns these six plants, whereas the alternative would be that someone else would own the plants.

Wire and cable is such a competitive industry that NTL has no special advantage that encourages it to produce in the U.S. and it is unable to sell into the U.S. Moving up the ladder of technological sophistication, one problem with exporting subscriber and switching equipment from Canada to the U.S. is the native-son purchasing policy of U.S. telephone companies, reinforced by Federal financing that is available at very low interest rates if equipment is manufactured in the U.S. A second problem is the U.S. tariff, and a third problem concerns the comparative costs of producing in Canada and the U.S. In fact, there are indications that NTL would not only find it impossible to export to the U.S. for cost reasons, but that it may also be cheaper to produce in the U.S. for the Canadian market. Thus Canada is losing neither jobs nor exports by the production of these items in the U.S., and the impact of NTL's investments in the U.S. is favourable to Canada.[13]

Digital switching is the most technically advanced area of production. The location of this activity in California, along with a research capacity, has been undertaken because this is recognized as the world's leading location for advanced telecommunications technology. By locating in California, NTL can interact directly with this research and can develop products for the U.S. markets, which will be the largest market and among the first markets to incorporate the new technology.

In recent years, the management of Northern Telecom has argued that the firm's long-term survival and growth will be contingent upon its ability to offer a broader range of innovative communications products. A convergence in the basic technology utilized in computers and telecommunications equipment, as well as increasingly geographic decentralization of data processing capability on user-access facilities, will make essential a competence in both product lines.[14] The implementation of a strategy to meet these requirements has been reflected not only in increased R&D expenditures, but also upon an outlay of $350 million during the 1970s for acquisitions, many of which were located in the United States. For example, during 1978, Northern Telecom purchased Danray Ltd., a Texas producer of computer-controlled switching networks, as well as Sycor Ltd. of Michigan and Data 100 Inc. of Minnesota, producers of remote information systems. Thus, part of Northern Telecom's investments abroad have involved the transfer of technology via acquisition to enhance its existing resources.

These moves represent a variation of the product cycle theory of international trade and investment. The theory, as applied to the U.S., shows the development of new products leading first to domestic sales, then to exports and finally to investment abroad. In the case of new technology involving digital switching, NTL has been developing it in part abroad, to be produced first abroad for the largest market that will use the new technology.

The case of NTL suggests that there is a favourable impact on Canada from its production in the U.S., because the alternative would be lost markets. The fact that there may be an unfavourable employment impact on Canada, if NTL services the Canadian market in the future from the U.S., is not due to NTL having plants in the U.S., but because of comparative cost conditions between Canada and the U.S. If NTL's U.S. plants do not sell into Canada at the expense of plants in Canada, then the alternative could be that another foreign firm would supply Canada from abroad in place of NTL. The realistic alternative is thus the Canadian consumer being supplied by some other plant in the U.S., as opposed to NTL's plant in the U.S., not the alternative of an NTL plant in Canada as opposed to an NTL plant in the U.S.

The foregoing example is not to suggest that all manufacturing investment abroad by Canadian firms has a favourable impact on Canada, but rather that this seems to be the case for the U.S. operations of NTL. In addition, the example suggests the type of analysis that needs to be undertaken, incorporating details of products, technology and markets, as well as proposing an appropriate alternative to which the situation should be compared.

Inco

Inco is a Canadian company with over 84,000 shareholders, 64% of whom have addresses in Canada and hold 48% of the outstanding shares, while 34% are U.S. residents and hold 37% of the shares. Thus 2% of the shareholders who are non North-American hold 15% of the shares. The company together with its subsidiaries

> . . .mines, refines and markets nickel in a variety of forms from Canadian ores. The Company also produces and markets from these same ores substantial amounts of copper and platinum-group metals, as well as iron ore, and limited quantities of cobalt, gold, silver, sulphur, selenium and tellurium. In addition, Inco produces and markets foundry additives and a wide range of nickel and high-nickel alloy rolling mill products. The Company is also actively engaged in the exploration for and development of new sources of nickel and other metals as well as other resources.[15]

As previously noted, through ESB Inc. in the United States, acquired in 1974 for $234 million, Inco is one of the world's major manufacturers of batteries and related products.[16]

In 1976, Inco had $2 billion U.S. in sales, $3.6 billion U.S. in assets and almost 56,000 employees (see Table 6, Chapter 2). The percentage distribution of foreign sales, assets and employees was as follows:

	Sales	Assets	Employees
	----------------------%----------------------		
Canada	11	53	46
United States	50	23	27
Other	39	24	27

Therefore, Inco's principal operating assets were located in North America, with over half of them in Canada and a high proportion of employees in Canada, although only 11% of sales were made in Canada.

Inco's output in terms of sales during 1978 could be classified as metal products 41%, batteries 38%, and other products 21% with refined nickel accounting for 47% of the metal products sales and 29% of total sales. In Canada, Inco is concerned primarily with mining, smelting and refining nickel and other metals as well as with conducting some of its research and exploration.

The foreign operations of Inco are situated primarily in the United States where, apart from marketing outlets and a research laboratory, the company has rolling mills making nickel alloys in all standard rolling mill forms through its ownership of Huntington Alloys Inc.,[17] and owns ESB Inc. which is a manufacturer of batteries and related products and itself has joint ventures in Sweden and India. In the U.K., Inco owns a rolling mill (Henry Wiggins & Co. Ltd.), a firm fabricating formed metal products (Daniel Doncaster & Sons Ltd.), a nickel refinery in Wales and a precious metal refinery at Acton.

During the 1970s, two major nickel projects were undertaken in Guatemala and Indonesia, and a seabed nodule mining operation had Japanese, German and U.S. investors in a joint venture with Inco. The nickel operations, owned 80% by Inco and 5% by Japanese investors in Indonesia were well under construction in 1975, and essentially completed in 1978 at a total project cost of $820 million, and a production capacity of 100 million pounds per year. The output was destined for Japan.[18] In Guatemala, the lateritic nickel project, owned 80% by Inco and 20% by Hanna Mining Inc. was halfway completed in 1975, and scheduled for completion in 1977, with an annual production rate of 28 million pounds of nickel contained in nickel matte, at an estimated total project cost of $24 million.[19] In general, exploration is undertaken by Inco on a worldwide, land and sea basis, wherever there appear to be good prospects for mineral discoveries.

Criticism in Canada has been directed at Inco's Indonesian and Guatemalan operations on the grounds that employment abroad is being substituted for employment in Inco's Canadian nickel operations.[20] In order to understand Inco's strategy behind these investments, it should be recalled that Inco's dominant global position in the nickel industry has been severely eroded since 1952, when the firm accounted for over 90% of the non-communist world's nickel needs, whereas the figure in 1975 was about 35%.[21]

Inco has mined sulphide (or Class I) nickel, a high purity material, at its facilities in Ontario and Manitoba, while its operations in Guatemala extract lateritic (Class II) nickel, which is less pure and contains ferronickel and sinter oxides. Class I nickel has been extensively utilized in electrolytic cathodes, but Class II nickel is required for the production of stainless steel. Between 1971 and 1976 demand for Class II nickel grew at 7.5% per annum, while the rate for Class I grew at 3.5%.[22] Thus, investment in different types of nickel ores becomes essential to meet shifts in market requirements.

Investment in Guatemala was also viewed by the company as one way of protecting its market position since lateritic nickel ore deposits are cheaper to mine, because they involve surface mining, as opposed to underground mining for the nickel sulphide deposits in Canada. However, lateritic deposits require considerable energy, oil-fired in the case of Guatemala, for drying and processing the deposits.

> Increased fuel oil prices affect the cost of producing nickel from laterites more than they affect the cost of producing it from sulfides. This occurs principally because fuel oil is used to dry wet lateritic ores (containing 25% moisture) and to generate electrical energy used to smelt the dried ores to matte or ferronickel, as is done in New Caledonia. On the other hand, nickel sulfide ores can be concentrated by flotation techniques, and nickel metal can be recovered with cheap hydroelectric energy, as is done in Canada and Norway.[23]

When the Guatemalan project was planned, oil prices were low and so the operation made economic sense — a fact which was altered once oil prices began to rise. However, the commitment had been made to develop the deposits and the project carried on. The case of the Guatemalan project illustrates the fact that mining developments require a long lead time.[24]

Investment in the Indonesian lateritic deposits was motivated by similar considerations, but with the additional fact that by being associated with Japanese investors, Inco would be able to penetrate the Japanese market both for sales of nickel and through forward integration for sales of processed metal products. Sales of nickel from Canada to Japan were limited by the Japanese tariff on refined nickel as opposed to the free entry of nickel in matte. In addition, the provincial government of Ontario, which had certain constitutional power over national resources, was reluctant in the early 1970s to give a long term committment to Inco to increase shipments of nickel in matte to Japan.[25]

Some of the output from Indonesia and Guatemala would be shipped to Inco's refinery in Wales for sale inside the European Economic Community. The Welsh refinery provided Inco with a position in this important market which could be lost to competitors without this presence. Thus, the offshore investments of Inco did not necessarily substitute for production from Canada since this may not have been a commercially viable alternative.

In the Indonesian and Guatemalan cases, it could be argued that, at the time, based on reasonable projections of cost and demand, Inco made a decision to protect its declining position in the world nickel market. If it had not invested in Indonesia, it is extremely unlikely that it would have been in a position to supply the Japanese market from Canada and thus no loss of Canadian employment was involved, and the Canadian balance of payments could expect to benefit in the long run from the investment. The investment in Guatemala, if it had not been made by Inco, would probably have been made by some other firm; if oil prices had not risen, Guatemalan nickel may have displaced Canadian nickel and employment in certain European markets, because costs of mining and processing were lower in Guatemala. Since the oil price increase, Canadian sulphide nickel deposits are more competitive with Guatemala than they might have been and so the displacement may not be as great. However, in general, it is difficult to argue that if Inco had not invested in Guatemala some other firm would not have done so. The question then becomes, is Canada better off with one of its firms as the developer or some foreign firm, because in either instance some Canadian nickel is likely to be displaced.

Inco's refinery in Wales and its rolling mills and metal fabrication plants in the U.S. and U.K. are aimed at servicing from within markets which are protected and where the alternative is likely to be no sales if exporting to these markets is attempted.

The case of investment in ESB Inc. presented a different set of circumstances, with Inco attempting to diversify its operations away from both Canada and nickel (and other metals).

> Also in 1974, the Company inaugurated a program to reduce dependence on its traditional business by diversifying into other fields. The Company entered into the packaged power industry with the acquisition of ESB Incorporated for $234 million, effective as of August 1, 1974.[26]
> . . . the basic objectives of the diversification program were: to spread our business risks with respect to both products and geography; and to increase growth in earnings and improve their quality and stability.[27]

The impact on Canada has to be measured relative to how the $234 million might have been spent if ESB Inc. had not been acquired. By selecting different hypothetical projects or industries as alternative investments in Canada, it would be possible to show different employment or balance of payments impacts on Canada. As it stands, ESB Inc. purchases very little from Inco in Canada so that the direct employment effect on Canada is minimal. Recoupment of the investment in Canada through dividend remittances in the balance of payments will depend on the profitability of ESB Inc. and its policy with respect to dividends versus reinvestment of retained earnings.

Inco presents a different set of circumstances to NTL, because of the differing nature of the two firms' operations and markets. Inco diversified away from its main area of expertise when it invested in the U.S., while NTL increased the scope of its existing telecommunications business. For NTL, it is clear that servicing the U.S. market through exports from Canada is not a feasible alternative, and so the impact on Canada of NTL's investment abroad is likely to be clearly favourable.

For Inco, investment in the foreign lateritic nickel deposits made commercial sense for the company, at least at the time the investment committment was made, and was likely to be in the interests of Canada as well. Unforeseen and changed circumstances may have reduced the favourable impact on Canada. Inco's investment in ESB Inc. was a different matter, and here it is possible to argue that Canada would have been better off with the same amount of investment being made in Canada as opposed to the U.S. However, to be fair in the comparison, it could also be argued that Canada might have benefited if NTL had diversified in Canada as opposed to investing in telecommunication manufacturing in the U.S. The alternative scenario chosen will determine the impact felt in Canada, and thus there are wide differences of opinion over the desirability of outward investment.

Alcan

Alcan Aluminium Ltd. (Alcan), in 1978, had assets of $4.6 billion and equity positions in over 100 companies in over 30 countries.[28] Sales in 1978 exceeded $4.6 billion and Alcan ranked as one of Canada's largest multinational corporations in terms of assets and sales.[29]

The percentage distribution of Alcan's domestic and foreign sales, assets and employees in 1976 were as follows:

	Sales	Assets	Employees
	%------------------------		
Canada	17	48	31
United States	21	9	6
United Kingdom	15	16	14
Other	47	27	49

An examination of Alcan's foreign investments revealed ownership of bauxite/alumina operations in Jamaica, Australia, Brazil and West Africa; smelting operations in the U.K., Scandinavia and Brazil; and aluminum fabrication operations in numerous countries and regions including the U.S., U.K., Europe, Latin America, Africa, Asia and the South Pacific. As previously observed, while about half of Alcan's assets were in Canada, approximately 70% of its employees and 83% of its sales were outside Canada. Alcan, as a vertically integrated aluminum company, relied entirely on foreign sources of supply for bauxite and alumina, and extensively on foreign markets for sales of aluminum ingot and fabricated aluminum products. The prime reason for the existence of an aluminum industry in Canada has been the availability of a plentiful supply of accessible energy, which is required in large quantities to produce aluminum ingot.

A continuing concern of Alcan is therefore that it should have access to both bauxite and markets for ingot. This has been achieved by establishing a wide variety of commercial arrangements, involving total or partial ownership of foreign bauxite sources, entrance into consortia or joint venture agreements for foreign bauxite, long term contractual arrangements and spot market purchases. In marketing ingot, Alcan makes short term and long term sales contracts with foreign customers, and has integrated forward into foreign markets in order to produce fabricated aluminum products for foreign customers. In sum, it is hardly an exaggeration to say that without Alcan's foreign involvements, there would be no Canadian aluminum industry, or its configuration would be so different from the present that it is difficult to speculate on an alternative scenario.

The case of Alcan's foreign investments illustrates that it is extremely difficult to assess the impact on the capital exporting country of all the firm's outward investment, but it is possible to discuss a particular investment or subset of investments. Thus an examination will be made of Alcan's decision after 1958 to invest (through vertical integration forward) in fabrication in the U.S. This decision represented a major strategic choice for Alcan, because of the circumstances in which it found itself.

Alcan's U.S. sales declined from 233,000 tons in 1956, to 100,000 tons in 1960, following its separation from Alcoa as a result of an American antitrust action. The management of Alcan concluded that:

> its role of aluminum ingot supplier to the world was a failure and it embarked on a longterm plan to pump millions of dollars into its own fabricating facilities around the world. The most significant of these major developments was the start of Alcan fabrication in the U.S. . . .[30]
>
> With insufficient captive outlets for its ingot, Alcan was in a particularly vulnerable position. The resulting challenge upon Alcan, as shareholders are aware, was to bolster the firm demand load on its Canadian smelters through the expansion of fabricating activities in markets where business could be created.[31]

As a result, in 1963, Alcan acquired its first aluminum fabricating plant in the U.S., and from then on, continued to expand by way of new investment and acquisition of U.S. fabricating facilities. By 1974, ingot and fabricated sales to third parties in the U.S. represented 27% of Alcan's worldwide sales (tons) of aluminum, and Alcan was established as a major fabricator in the U.S.: in fact, the largest aluminum company engaged primarily in fabricating in the U.S. Meanwhile, the ingot for its U.S. operations was purchased from its Canadian smelters.[32]

The choices facing Alcan after 1956 were fairly stark. Either it obtained outlets for its ingot on world markets and especially in the U.S., or it would have to become a supplier of ingot to non-integrated aluminum fabricators. Given that its major competitors were themselves integrating forward into fabrication, Alcan considered that it would be too vulnerable to remain primarily as an ingot supplier. The strategy of investing in U.S. fabrication facilities was dictated by the size of the market and the fact that U.S. tariffs on fabricated aluminum products were higher than on primary aluminum. The strategy has been successful to date and has allowed for expansion to occur in smelting capacity in Canada with the attendant economic benefits to Canada.

In sum, the alternative to investment in the U.S. by Alcan would almost certainly have been lost markets and unstable markets for ingot produced in Canada. The expansion of fabrication in Canada as opposed to the U.S. was not a realistic alternative, given the trade barriers that existed. Overall, this case of investment abroad by a Canadian firm has had a favourable impact on employment and the balance of payments in Canada, providing the suggested alternative scenarios are the ones which would have otherwise occurred.

SUMMARY OBSERVATIONS

The three cases of CDIA examined above have argued that there can be benefits to Canada from CDIA when the most likely alternative course of events would have rendered less benefits. It is not argued that all outward investment will be beneficial, but rather that, with the present state of knowledge and the limited number of cases examined, neither blanket approval nor condemnation is appropriate. The earlier contention is supported that case by case consideration of CDIA is required.

This need not be too onerous in Canada because of the small number of firms which account for a large proportion of the $14 billion of CDIA. However, even with a case by case approach, there will be no definitive answers about the extent of the impact on Canada, because there will be a range of reasonable alternative sets of circumstances that might have occurred. Once more experience has been gained in this type of analysis, it will be possible to narrow the range of alternatives and approach a more definitive evaluation. At present, public discussion is at the stage of making wild accusations based on sets of unstated but implicit assumptions about alternatives, that if they had existed, would support the accusation being made.

It is clear, however, that Canadian multinationals that make foreign investment decisions of a substantial size, which have a major employment impact, will have to inform the state about these decisions, because the consequences of the decision is that the rest of society has to pay for the relocation of resources, via unemployment insurance, loss of tax revenues, and regional subsidies. Corporations receive from the state the right to exist. A concomitant responsibility (up to now referred to as social responsibility re the lives of people affected by it), may have to be embodied in legislation, namely, that the state has the right to know about significant moves which firms intend to make before they make them. This, after all, is the philosophy of the FIRA. The process may be unpalatable for the state as well as for the company, for the state may have to accept the logic of the firm's actions in going abroad, which in turn may reflect on the state's inept management of the economy. At other times, the process may serve to highlight inept management in the corporation which has driven the firm to consider such action as investing abroad.

The alternative to a more formalized government/business dialogue on major investment decisions abroad is a continuing series of incidents, such as the Inco layoffs in 1978, which cumulate to the point where the demand for public action is so great, that real constraints are placed on corporations to the detriment of both the corporations and the economy.

Canadian public policy towards outward investment is outlined in Chapter 5. The present discussion suggests that any blanket policies promoting CDIA will lead to different impacts on Canada, depending on the nature of the investment undertaken. These policies often have some other objective in mind, such as promoting development in a less developed country. Secondly, the long standing encouragement by governments of Canadian firms to achieve better export performance will lead these firms to consider ways of servicing foreign markets. Sometimes this may be undertaken by exports from Canada, but at other times, the only alternative may be locating a plant in the foreign market. The whole issue of the limited size of the Canadian market for Canadian firms is then altered, because the market available to Canadian firms is the domestic market plus exports, and where exports are discouraged by tariff and non-tariff barriers, the domestic market plus the market serviced by a plant located abroad.

National governments may be increasingly brought into conflict with each other where special incentives and subsidies are given to foreign firms to locate within a particular state, and it is perceived by the capital exporting state to be a net loss of investment due to the subsidy. Such an irritant will increase if there are exports from the firm back to the capital exporting country, a situation which unions will watch carefully. Already in Canada, bidding is taking place between Ontario and

Quebec for a share of the large new investments which will be made by the U.S. automobile manufacturers. This bidding involves offers of financial assistance from the federal government which will sensitize the U.S. and other governments to the evolving situation. For this and other reasons connected with the politics of certain countries, foreign investment inward and outward is becoming an issue for foreign policy-making as well as for domestic economic policy.

NOTES

1. C.F. Bergsten, T. Horst, and T.H. Moran, *American Multinationals and American Interests,* (Washington: Brookings Institution, 1978), p. 450.

2. J. Niehans, "Benefits of Multinational Firms for a Small Parent Economy: The Case of Switzerland", in T. Agmon and C.P. Kindleberger, ed., *Multinationals from Small Countries,* (Cambridge: MIT Press, 1977), pp. 18-20.

3. Privy Council Office, *Foreign Ownership and the Structure of Canadian Industry,* (Ottawa: Queen's Printer, 1968), p. 353.

4. *Ibid.,* p. 350.

5. Privy Council Office, *Foreign Direct Investment in Canada,* (Ottawa: Information Canada, 1972), pp. 473-474.

6. See. R.J. Barnet and R.E. Muller, *Global Reach: The Power of the Multinational Corporations,* (New York: Simon and Schuster, 1974), pp. 303-308.

7. Relevant studies from the U.S. include:

J.N. Behrman, *Direct Manufacturing Investment, Exports and The Balance of Payments,* (New York: National Foreign Trade Council Inc., 1968).

R.B. Stobaugh, et al., *Nine Investments Abroad and their Impact at Home,* (Boston: Division of Research, Harvard Business School, 1976).

U.S. Tariff Commission, *Implications of Multinational Firms for World Trade and Investment and for U.S. Trade and Labour,* Report to the U.S. Senate and its Subcommittee on International Trade, (Washington: U.S. Government Printing Office, 1973).

G.S. Hufbauer and F.M. Allen, *Overseas Manufacturing Investment and the Balance of Payments,* (Washington: U.S. Treasury Dept., Tax Policy Research Studies, 1968).

Business International, *The Effects of U.S. Corporate Foreign Investment, 1960-1970, 1960-1972, 1970-73* (New York, Business International, 1975).

U.S. Chamber of Commerce, *Report on a Multinational Enterprise Survey 1960-1970,* (Washington: U.S. Chamber of Commerce, 1972). Lawrence G. Franko, *The European Multinationals* (Stamford, Conn.: Greylock Publishers, 1976).

Y. Tsurumi, *The Japanese are Coming: A Multinational Spread of Japanese Firms* (Cambridge: Ballinger, 1976); R. Vernon, *Storm over the Multinationals: The Real Issues,* (Cambridge: Harvard University Press, 1977).

R. Vernon, *The Economic and Political Consequences of Multinational Enterprise: An Anthology*, (Boston: Division of Research, Harvard Business School, 1972), a collection of previously published articles by Vernon.

M. Y. Yoshino, *The Japanese Multinational Enterprise: Strategy and Structure* (Cambridge: Harvard University Press, 1977).

C. F. Bergsten, T. Horst and T.H. Moran, *American Multinationals and American Interests*, (Washington: Brookings Institution, 1978).

W.B. Reddaway, *Effects of U.S. Direct Investment Overseas: Final Report* (Cambridge: Cambridge University Press, 1970); T.K. Houston and J.N. Dunning, *U.K. Industry Abroad*, (London: Financial Times, 1976).

8. K. Kojima, "International Impact of Foreign Direct Investment: A Japanese vs. an American Type", in *The Oriental Economist*, (December, 1973), pp. 28-31; Y. Tsurumi, *op. cit.*, pp. 75-82. This observation is not valid for much of Japan's overseas investment in manufacturing since 1973, i.e., investments in the U.S. to avoid protectionist counter measures.

9. Senate Subcommittee on Multinational Corporations of the Committee on Foreign Relations, *Multinational Corporations and United States Foreign Policy*, Washington: U.S. Government Printing Office, 1973, Part I, pp. 1-2.

10. *The Financial Post 500*, (Summer, 1979), p. 32.

11. Northern Telecom, *Annual Report 1978*, p. 11.

12. Science Council of Canada, *Annual Report 1976-1977*, (Ottawa: Supply and Services, 1977), p. 28.

13. Testimony of NTL to Senate of Canada Standing Committee on Foreign Affairs, 17 Nov., 1976, pp. 3:9 - 3:17.

14. *Annual Report 1978*, pp. 12-14.

15. Inco, *10-K Report, 1975*, p. 2.

16. Inco, *Annual Report, 1978*, pp. 9-10.

17. *Ibid.*, p. 12.

18. Inco, *10-K Report, 1975*, p. 8.

19. *Ibid.*, pp. 8-9.

20. See Submission from the United Steelworkers of America to the Select Committee of the Ontario Legislature on the Inco Layoffs, Dec., 1977.

21. Inco, *10-K Report*, (Securities and Exchange Commission, 1975), pp. 9-10.

22. Wood Gundy estimates.

23. Bureau of Mines, U.S. Department of the Interior, Nickel — 1977, Mineral Commodity Profiles MCP-4, (July, 1977), p. 14.

24. One observer suggests that the decisions to go ahead with the Indonesian and Guatemalan projects were made during the optimism which existed 10 to 15 years ago in the 1960s.

25. Statement by Inco Limited to a Select Committee of the Ontario Legislature, 20 December, 1977 (mimeo, 1977), p. 30.

26. *Ibid.*, p. 17.

27. *Financial Post*, 2 Oct., 1976, p. 41.

28. Alcan Aluminium Ltd., *Annual Report 1978*, p. 43.

29. *The Financial Post 500,* (Summer, 1979), p. 8. Rank figures include crown corporations.

30. Albert W. Whitaker, *Aluminum Trail,* (Montreal: Alcan Press, 1974), p. 343.

31. N.V. Davis, "Alcan now Stronger, Sounder after Decade of Growth, Change", *The Compass,* (June, 1967), p. 4.

32. In 1977, Alcan attempted to acquire the aluminum smelting operation of Revere Copper and Brass Inc. in Alabama. This was blocked by the U.S. Department of Justice. It would have represented Alcan's first source of primary aluminum in the U.S.

Chapter 5

In Search of a Policy

Canadian government policy towards CDIA has evolved over time at both the federal and provincial levels. Until recently, the federal government neither actively promoted nor discouraged such investment, and was involved essentially only in handling problem situations that arose. For example, the government became involved in negotiations concerning the nationalization of assets in the USSR, in the Commercial Debts Agreement with Cuba, and with lump sum settlements with east European states, some of which involved Canadian investment, but most of which dealt with the assets of Canadian immigrants. While the negotiations, which were essentially handled by the Department of External Affairs, were a reactive type of policy, the Department of Industry, Trade and Commerce was the locus for policies promoting CDIA.

It was not until 1967, however, that a major official statement was made on the subject. In a speech to an international development seminar, the Minister of Trade and Commerce stated:

> from now on our officials at home and throughout the world are instructed to assist businessmen in respect of proposed investments and indeed actively to bring foreign investment opportunities to the attention of Canadian firms, whenever this appears to be in our national interest.

Mr. Winters went on to say, that at the time, the Canadian government was

> exploring a number of other techniques to encourage Canadian private investment in developing countries, including the possible introduction of a plan to insure Canadian investors against some of the special risks inherent in productive ventures in developing countries.[1]

Prior to this date, the policy of the department had been to promote the export of goods from Canada for reasons of balance of payments, economic growth, and employment. It was considered counterproductive for Canadian trade commissioners to promote Canadian investment abroad, because to do so was seen as exporting Canadian jobs. This attitude to export orientation has died hard within the department, and it has only been recently that trade commissioners have been allowed to comment on investment opportunities abroad for Canadian firms, in the event that a foreign market could not be served by Canadian exports. In 1974, the Minister of Industry, Trade and Commerce made a speech suggesting the desirability of Canadian firms becoming involved in joint ventures abroad with foreign firms.[2] The joint venture approach reflects the preference which the Canadian government has for promoting local equity participation in foreign firms in Canada, a policy being actively encouraged through the Foreign Investment Review Agency.

In general, an appreciation of the Canadian government's policy and attitude towards direct investment abroad requires an understanding of Canada's position as a major capital importer. Canada did not sign the Code of Liberalization of Capital Movements of the Organization for Economic Cooperation and Development because the code was influenced by capital-exporting countries and was not seen to recognize Canada's position as a major capital importer.[3] In addition, Canada was the only OECD country not to sign the convention that established the International Centre for Settlement of Investment Disputes (ICSID), an agency of the World Bank. There are two reasons for the abstention; first, Canada's concern as a capital importer, and second, a concern that a Canadian provincial government might become involved in a dispute, and it might be outside the jurisdiction of the federal government to sign a convention affecting provincial interests, especially where natural resources are concerned.

The tendency to abstain was broken in the summer of 1976 when Canada signed an OECD code which concerned itself with capital exporting activities. On June 21, 1976, the annual ministerial meeting of the OECD council gave approval to a "code of conduct for multinational enterprises." While the code was voluntary and not mandatory, it was expected to enjoy political and moral weight. The code was but one part of an OECD investment package of documents which also presented a framework of government responsibilities for fair treatment of the MNCs. In this instance, the OECD member states agreed that the treatment of MNCs under laws, regulations and administrative practices should be no less favourable than that accorded in like situations to domestic enterprises.

However, the contents of the OECD code had to be modified before the Canadian government would sign it; specifically, the government was not willing to accept the principle of automatically according national treatment to foreign owned enterprises in Canada. Nonetheless, the change in Canada's perception of itself as a capital importing, as well as capital exporting nation, cannot be underestimated.

EXPORT DEVELOPMENT CORPORATION

In recent years, government support of CDIA has been primarily carried out through the activities of two agencies. The first, and most significant agency, is the Export Development Corporation (EDC), which was created in 1968 to supercede the Export Credit Corporation originally established in 1944. The EDC was created "for the purposes of facilitating and developing trade between Canada and other countries."[4] As a wholly-owned federal corporation, it is a commercially self-sustaining enterprise which has consistently operated at a profit, rather than being an aid-granting agency. Although it initially raised funds by borrowing from the Consolidated Revenue Fund of Canada, all of the EDC's monetary requirements are now met by borrowing from private sources.

The EDC provides long term loans to foreign purchasers of Canadian capital and technical services, export credit insurance against non-payment for Canadian firms, and surety insurance for exporters who must post performance bonds.

In particular, since 1969, the EDC has offered an insurance scheme to Canadian firms intending to make offshore investments in the form of the Foreign Investment Guarantee Programme. Under the provisions of this service, "any person, partnership, corporation, government agency or other legal entity carrying on business or other activities in Canada" can apply to the EDC for a guarantee against "certain defined political risks" for proposed foreign investments.[5] The programme is aimed at helping Canadian companies retain a strong competitive position relative to firms supported by equivalent schemes offered by the governments of other developed countries, as well as encouraging industrial growth in the investor and recipient countries.

Eligibility of applicants for protection has been determined by four conditions:

(a) *Nature of Investment* — The statutory objectives set forth in the EDC's enabling legislation direct the programme to facilitate the movement of Canadian goods and services abroad, and the utilization of "Canadian capital and skills in a manner which contributes to the economic and social progress of Canada and host countries."[6] Consequently, protection has been available for new investments only, although in recent years, the EDC has been prepared to include in its definition of new investments, a significant expansion, modernization, or development of existing enterprises.

The programme is meant to cover most of the rights which a potential investor might acquire in an offshore investment such as equity, loans, management contracts, royalty and licensing agreements. Potential investments may be in the form of cash, contributions in kind, or financial guarantees. However, ineligible proposals include loans to foreign governments, investments only in land, portfolio and short-term investments, or the takeover of foreign firms. Investments can be made directly in foreign enterprises or indirectly via related companies in Canada, the host country or a third nation.

(b) *Size and Area of Investment* — The EDC provides limited protection for investments in developing countries, and has reserved the option to restrict insurance coverage in any country at any time. While the EDC has stated that it will consider proposals for investment regardless of their size, the amount it will offer has been constrained by geographic factors or the size of practical business operations. To date, the size of investments insured under the programme has varied from $45,000 to $14 million. More than half of the approved proposals have been made by small businesses, with investments of less than $1 million in size.[7]

(c) *Economic benefit* — Proposed investments must provide some identifiable economic advantage to Canada, such as the sale of capital goods and services abroad, the earning of foreign exchange, or the establishment of sources of raw materials which are not currently available in Canada. Similarly, investments must provide a significant positive influence upon the host economy, especially with regard to the development of a self-sustaining private sector. These benefits would normally include the expansion of employment, improvements in personnel skills or production techniques, and increases in the general standard of living of the recipient nation.

Not surprisingly, the EDC has stressed the inclusion of transfers of technical know-how in foreign direct investment packages, as well as the use of joint venture enterprises in partnership with local entrepreneurs. The EDC has tended to favour proposals from Canadian owned firms, since these companies have been more likely to purchase goods and services from Canadian sources than the subsidiaries of foreign owned corporations.

(d) *Host Government Attitudes* — Before the EDC will issue an insurance contract, the Canadian investor must secure a formal approval from the host government for the proposed activity of the foreign enterprise and for the investment by the Canadian firm in that project. Moreover, a host government must indicate its willingness to permit the repatriation of capital and the remittance of earnings, since the terms of the EDC's insurance do *not* protect potential investors from the effect of any exchange regulations or practices in existence at the time of the execution of a contract.

In a number of countries, the Canadian federal government has entered into bilateral agreements in which host nations acknowledge, in writing, the EDC's rights in regard to EDC insured investments. That is, they acknowledge that agreements are in effect by which the EDC, if necessary, would be subrogated to an insured investor's property and rights in these nations as protected by EDC guarantees.

Finally, investors are responsible for the study of host government laws and regulations dealing with foreign investment, as well as meeting all local disclosure requirements.

The EDC insurance programme is meant to provide protection for a Canadian investor against three basic types of non-commercial political risk:

(a) *Expropriation* — Some government actions may block the transmission of monies owed to an investor, prevent the disposition of sureties and rights accruing from the investment, or render impossible the exercise of effective control over the use or disposition of a significant portion of the investor's property.

(b) *Inconvertibility* — Host governments by action or inaction may prevent, for a specified period, the conversion of local currencies into Canadian dollars, or permit conversion only at a discriminatory rate.

(c) *Political Violence* — Injuries may occur to the physical condition of an investor's property, directly caused by war (whether or not by formal declaration), by hostile acts by any nation or internationally organized force, or by revolution or insurrection. Similar problems may occur in the hindering, combat of, or defence against expected hostile acts. Contracts do not include injuries or destruction of property caused by civil strife of a lesser degree than revolution or insurrection, but do include those derived from hostile incidents such as acts of sabotage by organized revolutionary or insurgent forces.

Needless to say, protection is not provided against those risks which would be encountered domestically, such as basic casualty risks like fire, flood, and storm-related damages, or from commercial problems such as inflation and a failure to make a profit. Similarly, coverage is not available against currency fluctuations.

Under the EDC scheme, insured clients can secure protection for 85% of capital investments less than, and 75% for those greater than, $10 million. The EDC will provide insurance for up to 150% of the value of original equity investments for each of the three categories of non-commercial risk. The incremental sum provides coverage for retained earnings up to 50% of the original investments. Insurance for debt investments covers the outstanding amount of principal as well as any accrued unpaid interest up to 150% of the original transaction. Costs to investors have averaged 0.7% of the value of these investments on an annual basis. Readers should refer to Appendix A for a more detailed illustration of this programme.

Examples of the EDC's role in support of CDIA are numerous. One Canadian electronics manufacturer established a wholly owned subsidiary in Asia to provide a source of electronic components at lower labour and resource costs. Local entrepreneurs will, over time, acquire an interest in the enterprise. A management contract, a guarantee of debt repayment and the equity investment were all insured by EDC, thereby assisting the firm to retain a competitive position in its industry. Similarly, McCain Foods Ltd. has used the EDC to insure its food processing plant in Spain, while Lockheed Petroleum Services secured protection for its development of an undersea oil gathering and production system in Brazilian waters. A Canadian biological laboratory had the equity investments in three Latin American joint ventures insured by EDC, thereby permitting it to maintain and expand in local markets, which could no longer be served by direct exports.

No investments were insured by EDC during the first two years of the programme, since there was a requirement that insurance could only be purchased in those countries with which Canada had a bilateral investment protection treaty or agreement. The developing countries showed a strong reluctance to sign such treaties, partly because it implied that they were poor insurance risks. An amendment to the EDC Act in 1971 removed this requirement, substituting the current requirement of host government approval. The value of the investments insured by the EDC mushroomed from $43 million in 1974, to $121 million in 1976, and to $202 million in 1978. The EDC estimated that during 1976, the $121 million worth of insured risks resulted in accompanying sales from Canada of $142 million in capital equipment, sales of $328 million in components and raw materials, $78 million in technical and management services, $88 million in fees from royalties, licensing, and leasing agreements, and the repatriation to Canada of $194 million in dividends and interest. In total, EDC claimed that there was approximately an $830 million favourable contribution to the Canadian balance of payments.[8]

As shown in Table 1, EDC insurance protection has been oriented for proposed investments in developing countries with support principally given to those in the Middle East, Latin America, and Western Africa. Table 2 indicates that guarantees had been primarily oriented to resource, food, beverage and pharmaceutical industries. Only a small amount of support had been given to proposals involving secondary manufacturing or service industries.

The government's investment insurance scheme differs from many types of commercial insurance. First, the limitation on new investments discriminates against existing offshore investments. Clients must advise the EDC on all of their existing foreign holdings and activities before they are able to secure a contract. Second, the seller (government) has considerable discretion as to whether it sells the insurance or not, even if it is a new investment in a developing country. Third, the insurance facility may well be withdrawn in the event that a country causes a claim to be made for a non-commercial political risk. In the event of such a claim, the government may refuse to sell further insurance for that country; thus, the scheme would only operate on a long-term basis providing no claim was ever made. The investment insurance programme may, however, act as a deterrent to a country contemplating nationalization.

Moreover, while the types of non-commercial political risks for which insurance can be bought — nationalization, war, and currency convertibility — are typical of the risks which may be experienced, the insurance programme may ignore another important set of risks, those associated with various forms of wealth deprivation brought about by host government policies. There are many ways in which a government can hinder the exploitation or use of assets within its jurisdiction, such as discriminatory tariffs and taxation, refusal to issue visas for the entry of key technical personnel, refusal to permit the sale of goods, services, and assets, and refusal to permit the mining of discovered ore bodies. An example of the latter occurred in Australia, where Noranda discovered a uranium deposit, and the Australian government refused to issue the export permits necessary for the development and commercialization of the deposits. In the event that these types of risks cannot be insured, the investor is forced to make his own arrangements. This has in fact occurred, and is exemplified by an American firm, Kennecott Corporation, in Chile. This company reduced the risks of its operation by factoring its sales contracts to European and Japanese banks, so that in the event of nationalization, the host government had to deal not only with the United States government, but also with the Japanese and a number of European governments and financial institutions as well.[9]

CANADIAN INTERNATIONAL DEVELOPMENT AGENCY

The second agency by which the Canadian government has taken some steps to encourage CDIA has been the Canadian International Development Agency (CIDA). In 1960, an Order-in-Council created the External Aid Office which was responsible for the following: the operation and administration of all assistance programmes for which the Department of External Affairs received funds from parliament, the coordination of operations with other involved government agencies and ministries, and the direction of all Canadian efforts aimed at obtaining aid for developing countries affected by disasters.

In 1968, the name of the agency was changed to CIDA, and it was given the official mission of supporting:

> the efforts of developing countries in fostering their economic growth and the evolution of their social systems in a way that will produce a wide distribution of the benefits of development among the populations of these countries, enhance the quality of life and improve the capacity of all sectors of their population to participate in national development efforts.[10]

This goal was to be accomplished by the support of programmes of the United Nations and other international institutions, efforts to alleviate hunger, the provision of economic and social development assistance, the undertakings of the private sector in development cooperation, and the development of the productive capacity of developing countries.[11]

In 1970, in order to carry out these latter objectives, CIDA estab-

Table 1

EXPORT DEVELOPMENT CORPORATION: FOREIGN INVESTMENT GURANTEE CONTRACTS BY GEOGRAPHIC LOCATION, 1978 $THOUSANDS

Area	For Investment Guarantees	%	Total EDC Business*	%
Far East Asia	15,479	7.65	288,387	4.22
Middle East Asia	53,391	26.38	1,471,241	21.53
West Africa	22,522	11.13	64,019	0.94
North Africa	7,485	3.70	1,834,351	26.85
South and East Africa	6,618	3.27	96,492	1.41
Western Europe	14,686	7.26	638,964	9.35
Eastern Europe	—	—	1,735,180	25.39
U.S.A., Central America & Caribbean	38,735	19.14	438,680	6.42
Eastern South America	42,089	20.80	223,307	3.27
West South Africa	1,360	0.67	42,428	0.62
Total	202,365	100.00	6,833,049	100.00

* Includes loans and related guarantees, credit insurance and related guarantees, and foreign investment guarantees.
Source: Export Development Corporation, Annual Report, 1978, (Ottawa, 1979), p. 34.

Table 2

EXPORT DEVELOPMENT CORPORATION: FOREIGN INVESTMENT GUARANTEE CONTRACTS BY INDUSTRIAL SECTOR, 1978

Sector	$Millions	%
Food, Beverage and Pharmaceuticals	71,030	35.1
Resource and Primary Manufacturing	35,414	17.5
Oil and Gas	54,032	26.7
Service Industries	11,130	5.5
Tourism	6,678	3.3
Secondary Manufacturing	24,081	11.9
Total	202,365	100.00

Source: Export Development Corporation, Annual Report, 1978, (Ottawa, 1979), p. 54.

lished an Industrial Cooperation Programme which officially was meant to

> promote industrial growth in less developed countries of the world through the transfer of investment capital, technology, and management in joint venture projects.[12]

CIDA's Business and Industry division would provide grants of up to $10,000 for a starter study in which a potential investor could investigate an investment opportunity on site by sending representatives to the developing country. Firms may have subsequently appled for a grant of up to $100,000 to finance a more detailed feasibility study which was conducted on a shared (50/50) cost basis.

The division has sponsored promotional meetings in Canada to bring together foreign government representatives and the managers of Canadian firms, and compiled data on the potential interests of investors, as well as the investment climate in selected countries. CIDA's projects are primarily carried out by private contractors, consultants, suppliers and manufacturers in Canada.

Nonetheless, the support for CDIA by CIDA has been quite limited. As shown in Table 3, the initiatives for Canadian foreign investment in developing countries represented less than one-tenth of 1% of the federal government's outlays for development assistance between 1976 and 1978. Between 1970 and 1978, approximately 150 starter studies and 45 feasibility studies were authorized. Only 14 joint ventures were actually undertaken involving an aggregate offshore employment of 3,000 persons, and based on previous CIDA estimates, were probably worth less than $10 million.[13]

The former President of CIDA, Mr. Michel Dupuy, has acknowledged that "Canadian business is not taking full advantage of the opportunities offered by the various levels of government", and has attributed this situation, in part, to a failure to communicate information about government incentive programmes.[14] But the problem is also attitudinal in nature, since CIDA has tended to advance its industrial cooperation programme on moral and humanitarian grounds. Mr. Dupuy has declared that

> CIDA's motivation for industrial cooperation lies in providing assistance to countries in need . . . Business, *per se*, is not CIDA's business![15]

Appeals for participation by business consequently tend to stress the benefits for the general north-south relationship rather than corporate strategic and profit considerations. Not surprisingly, greater emphasis is given to direct nutritional, educational and financial assistance schemes.

CIDA also tends to discriminate heavily in favour of small to medium-sized firms, although these companies might reasonably be expected to favour the closer, larger and more familiar markets of the

United States and the E.E.C. The agency's insistence upon a 51% Canadian ownership requirement for applicants seeking investment incentives and contracts for development work may serve as another factor limiting the use of the programme.

OTHER GOVERNMENT DEPARTMENTS

As well as these activities of the federal government, other departments play a role in CDIA, such as the Departments of Finance and National Revenue with respect to taxation of foreign income and tariffs, the Department of Energy, Mines and Resources, and the Department of Manpower and Immigration. Provincial governments have also been involved. For a number of years, the government of Ontario has promoted joint ventures abroad involving Ontario based companies. In 1971, for example, the Ontario Department of Trade and Development sponsored a conference entitled "Establishing Licensing, Joint-Ventures and Branch Plants Abroad."

There is a clear distinction between the policy issues for Canada emanating from CDIA in developed and developing countries. While developing countries are the recipients of about one-quarter of CDIA, the problems generated by this investment are far more politically visible and account for by far the largest part of the time which government officials must spend on matters relating to investment abroad. These problems tend to be related to those activities associated with non-commercial risks. In developed countries the main issue areas tend to relate to taxation, tariffs and transfer pricing, antitrust, balance of payments, freedom to export, and the financing of monetary flows. The government has placed surprisingly little emphasis on requiring reciprocal treatment for Canadian foreign investors. Thus, for example, the Canadian government has not pressed for treatment in Japan for Canadian investors equivalent to that granted Japanese investors in Canada (for example, with respect to ease of entry and non-tariff barriers). Given Canada's openness to foreign investment, a public statement of the requirement for reciprocal treatment for Canadian investors abroad would have been, at the very least, a strong signal of encouragement to would-be Canadian investors.

The reluctance of the Canadian government to take a more positive attitude to CDIA, at least until recently, is all the more surprising given the repeated public statements about the drawbacks to Canadian firms in servicing a small (Canadian) market, compared with markets open to firms in the United States or in the European Economic Community. While exports are one way of gaining access to larger markets, foreign investment is an alternative, as United States firms have shown in Europe. A combined strategy of servicing foreign markets via trade and/or investment would at least have been worth discussing. It might be

Table 3

CANADIAN GOVERNMENT OFFICIAL DEVELOPMENT
ASSISTANCE DISBURSEMENTS BY PROGRAM, 1976—1978

1975-76 to 1977-78 ($ Millions)

	1975-76	1976-77	1977-78
Multilateral			
General UN Funds	28.00	34.25	45.50
Renewable Natural Resources	5.78	5.15	17.36
Population and Health	8.82	10.42	12.37
Education	.41	.50	.43
Commonwealth and Francophone Programs	4.64	5.17	7.97
Refugee and Relief	2.93	3.10	4.27
Trade Promotion	.38	.50	.50
Development Banks	2.19	4.22	.22
Other Programs	3.36	1.15	1.13
Multilateral Food Aid	103.22	87.21	91.27
Loans and Advances to International Financial Institutions	158.83	264.96	229.22
Sub-total	318.56	416.63	410.24
Bilateral			
Technical Assistance	52.34	61.03	54.63
Economic Assistance (Exclusive of Food Aid)	350.07	261.32	355.27
Bilateral Food Aid	119.32	149.44	139.08
Commonwealth Scholarships and Fellowships	1.99	1.94	1.88
International Emergency Relief	2.00	4.00	2.00
Sub-total	525.71	477.73	552.86

Other Programs

Non-Governmental Organizations	31.86	37.31	44.31
Other Food Aid Programs	—	.86	1.67
International Development Research Centre	27.00	29.70	34.50
Incentives to Canadian Private Investment in Developing Countries	.11	.93	.25
Canadian Scholarship Program	.27	.18	.23
Contribution to Italian Earthquake Reconstruction	—	—	1.00
Sub-total	59.24	68.98	81.96
Forgiveness of Loans to Least Developed Countries	—	—	231.89
Total	903.51	963.34	1276.95

In 1977-78, ODA expenditures of $1276.95 million included $231.89 million which covered the write-off of loans to least developed countries approved by Parliament in Supplementary Estimates B. Therefore the actual ODA expenditures, on a comparable basis with prior years amount to $1045.06 million.

Source: CIDA, *Annual Review 1977-78,* (Ottawa, 1978), p. 33.

argued that this strategy would be constrained by the high level of foreign investment in Canada, which meant that foreign owned firms would not view their Canadian operations as an appropriate base for investment in third countries. There are, however, significant existing exceptions to this thesis. For example, the separation of Alcan from Alcoa left Alcan with substantial overseas investments and markets. Ford Canada became the parent to many of Ford's Commonwealth investments, and other foreign companies used their Canadian operation to obtain preferential access to Commonwealth markets by way of trade and investment.

The *Canadian Forum* version of the Gray Report on foreign investment in Canada alluded to problems associated with the promotion of Canadian multinational companies:

> There are, at present, a number of Canadian controlled multinational companies headquartered in Canada, e.g., the banks, Alcan, Polymer (now Polysar), Massey Ferguson, MacMillan Bloedel, Moore Corporation, Seagrams and Crush International . . .
>
> From the point of view of Canadian interests, experience to date with Canadian multinationals has not been entirely satisfactory. There appears to be a tendency for Canadian companies that become more international during their maturation to become less Canadian to the point where, in some instances, their Canadian identity becomes nominal, e.g., Inco and Massey Ferguson. Trying to draw up a list of important Canadian MNEs underscores the problem. For example, are Alcan and Seagrams really Canadian controlled? The large and powerful U.S. market is a constant attraction for Canadian direct investment. Even Polymer, a Government owned corporation, has considered establishing a major expansion of its Sarnia operations in the U.S. Polymer has pointed to the need for a major facility within the large U.S. market (i.e. to be in the market), the possibility of supplying materials under U.S. aid programmes, and the insurance against possible U.S. governmental actions which could affect North American marketing operations.[16]

As pointed out in Chapter 2, in 1976, Massey-Ferguson had 92% of its total sales outside Canada, Moore 90%, Alcan 85%, International Nickel 89%, and MacMillan Bloedel 76%. These companies, which do have multinational status, have had to expand abroad in order to survive and grow in the global market place. Unfortunately, this strategy, necessary for global survival, has resulted in these companies becoming viewed by Canadian policy makers as non-Canadian. At present, the Canadian government appears to be following a shortsighted policy with respect to CDIA, in stark contrast to those pursued by governments such as those of Switzerland and Sweden.

CASE EXAMPLES

The following cases illustrate the position taken by the Canadian government with respect to problems arising from CDIA and some of the resulting implications.

Nationalization of Alcan's Operations in Guyana

In 1971, the Guyanese government nationalized the Demerara Bauxite Company (Demba), a wholly owned subsidiary of Alcan Ltd. Alcan's main smelter in Arvida, Quebec, was almost totally dependent on Guyanese bauxite, while its smelter in Kitimat, B.C., received Guyanese bauxite during the winter months. The communities of Arvida and Kitimat, with populations of 14,000 and 8,500 respectively, were supported by the aluminum operations. In addition, Alcan was a major exporter of aluminum both in absolute terms and relative to its total output. Even on these scant details, it can be argued that there might be significant repercussions in Canada from the nationalization, which would warrant concern on the part of the government.

However, the Canadian government chose to take a detached position during the negotiations as the following statement of Senator Martin demonstrates:

> I indicated, of course, that what the government of Guyana did in the exercise of its sovereign right was a matter for its own decision. Canadians would expect that their corporate nationals would be treated justly and in a non-discriminatory way.[17]

The attitude of the government is summed up in a statement by the Minister of Industry, Trade and Commerce on the day Guyana decided to nationalize Demba:

> We put the case that we expect Canadian companies not to be discriminated against in these matters. That is about the extent of what we can do in these matters.[18]

This attitude encouraged Alcan to seek support from American government and business interests in negotiating its case with the Guyanese government. The implications of this event, which have been examined in detail elsewhere,[19] were widespread, affecting CDIA, the large international aluminum firms, and host countries. However, it is the implications for Canada, involving CDIA both present and future, which will be examined here.

A *hands-off* stand on the part of the government has the effect of further discouraging CDIA, at least from a Canadian base of operation. Companies in Canada may therefore choose to invest abroad from subsidiary operations in countries where they can count on more positive government backing. Since the Canadian government does not at present subscribe to the requirement of prompt, adequate and effective compensation for nationalized assets, Canadian companies are reluctant to rely on governmental support. Suspicion is also aroused about the government's request for non-discriminatory treatment for Canadian assets, for the only other foreign bauxite producer in Guyana, Reynolds (a United States company), was not nationalized until nearly four years later, during which time no official protest was made by Canada about discriminatory treatment.

The response of foreign countries to Canada's position to date is difficult to determine. Certainly there is no reason for the countries to anticipate a harsh response from the Canadian government in the event of their introducing tough policies towards Canadian investment. It may be too extreme to suggest that foreign countries have been encouraged to nationalize Canadian assets, but at least the governmental constraints appear to be minimal.

It might be argued that the Alcan case is unique, and not sufficiently representative of future cases that are likely to occur. For example, the company was ambivalent in its attitude towards the need for government assistance during the early stages of the negotiations and may have requested help at too late a point in the discussions, but the Alcan affair illustrates two important issues.

First, it is clear that instances of foreign nationalization will always involve the government and will leave some impression about Canada in the minds of foreign governments, whether the Canadian government intervenes or not. If intervention occurs then any effective government assistance to corporations must be based on a degree of trust and mutual respect of government for corporations and vice versa. At present that respect is shallow, and this undermines one aspect of the management of foreign economic and political relations.

The second issue concerns the repercussions on Canada (and any capital exporting country) of close involvement with the overseas operations of Canadian companies. There is little doubt that the actions of International Telephone and Telegraph (ITT) in Chile symbolizes for many developing countries the involvement of the United States government in their domestic affairs through the company's operations. Any close corporate/capital exporting government relationship is likely to be viewed as foreign interference in domestic affairs. It is therefore surprising that some host governments have argued that the capital exporting governments should control the activities of their corporations in the host countries. The point here is that a government may be damned by the developing country if it does and damned if it does not seek to influence the foreign activities of its corporations.

The United States Senate has been critically examining the relationships which develop between a home government and its multinationals, as a result of policies such as the Overseas Private Investment Corporation (OPIC) which to a degree have been promoted by the need of the developing countries for capital. The result of OPIC has been to create a financial stake on the part of the government of the United States in privately owned American properties abroad which has consequences for American foreign policy. Because of recent cases, questions are being raised about the desirability of promoting United States investment abroad.[20]

The United Nations Group of Eminent Persons (GEP) Report[21] has attempted to come to grips with this issue by proposing that host countries state specificially the terms on which they welcome new foreign investment and how they expect such investment to operate. At the same time, the report proposes that home countries refrain from using companies as instruments for the attainment of foreign policy goals[22] and encourages the companies to act responsibly. Undoubtedly home governments will become involved in future issues and it is going to require fine judgment to decide when a corporation deserves assistance, for example, deciding when a host country is making unreasonable demands and when a company is behaving unreasonably.

International law is of limited assistance in these cases, because although principles and precedents exist, there is limited scope for enforcing decisions if countries choose not to cooperate. A prime example is Jamaica's membership of ICSID and that government's refusal to be bound by the convention when a dispute arose between it and the international aluminum companies.

Companies of Convenience — International Petroleum Corporation and Barcelona Traction

Just as the state of Delaware in the United States provides benefits to those incorporating in that state, so countries can provide benefits to companies incorporating within their jurisdiction. Often these benefits are financial, perhaps associated with taxation or currency convertibility; sometimes the benefits are associated with the ability to sustain secrecy about the nature of the firm's operations, as in the case of tax revenue. The result of these conveniences is that a company may be set up in Canada (or another country), and this company may in turn own operations abroad, but there may be little or no Canadian investment in the company. Essentially this is the case with the International Petroleum Corporation (IPC) and Barcelona Traction.

IPC was a wholly owned subsidiary of Exxon (then Standard Oil of New Jersey) which was nationalized by the Peruvian government. Since IPC's registered head office was in Toronto, the Peruvian government refused to deal diplomatically or legally with the United States government, stating that it was the Canadian government's concern. Canada was thus drawn into a dispute over a company which was located in Canada largely for reasons of convenience. However, Exxon does have substantial investments in Canada through its majority ownership and control of Imperial Oil which provided a dimension not present in the second case.

The Barcelona Traction case[23] involved the liquidation by the Spanish government of a hydroelectric company which was a subsidiary of Barcelona Light and Power Co. Ltd., a company incorporated in Canada, but 88% owned by Belgian nationals and less than 0.2% by Canadian nationals. The International Court of Justice considered this case and decided that it need not rule on the merits of the case itself, accepting the Spanish government's objection that the Belgian government had no legal capacity to espouse the claim, even though its nationals ultimately owned most of the company. It ruled that Barcelona Traction was a juristic entity registered in Canada, so that the right to espouse the claim rested solely with the Canadian government. The Canadian government chose not to do so at the legal level because there is no link of compulsory jurisdiction between Canada and Spain. At the political level the Canadian government agreed to try to bring together the parties, the Canadian receiver-manager and the Spanish company, to determine if some out-of-court settlement might be reached.

These two cases indicate how a third country, in this instance Canada, can be drawn into a dispute involving two other countries. As long as incorporation laws permit companies incorporated in Canada (and elsewhere) to operate in any line of business and in any part of the world, without reporting this to the incorporating jurisdiction, then any number of such surprise situations may arise for governments. It should be noted that the first attempt in Canada to control the expansion activities of firms has been proposed with respect to the future operations of the Foreign Investment Review Agency. This agency has the power to decide whether an existing foreign owned firm is to be allowed to expand its activities into different fields.[24]

Canada is not the only country in which these situations are likely to arise, so that there is an opportunity for the development of international understanding, if not an international agreement, on how such disputes should be arbitrated. But although agreement at the international level may be possible between developed countries, it is unlikely that developing countries would feel that they would derive much benefit from being party to such an agreement.

The United Nations GEP report makes an interesting recommendation on this score:

> The Group recommends that, in such contexts, home countries should refrain from involving themselves in differences and disputes between multinational corporations and host countries. If serious damage to their nationals is likely to arise they should confine themselves to normal diplomatic representations. No attempt should be made to use international agencies as means of exerting pressure.[25]

While this recommendation relates to disputes, in general involving multinational corporations and host governments, it would cover the situation involving corporations of convenience. In this respect, the recommendation is somewhat naive in that it expects home countries to act as bystanders and take no action outside of normal diplomatic representations to assist the owners of their corporations. Obviously the case of ITT in Chile was uppermost in the minds of the group, but a general view pervades the report that multinational corporations can divorce themselves from the politics of the environment in which they operate and that, if they did, such disputes would not arise. This is a purist view with no substance in fact, when it is recognized that developing countries especially make demands on multinational corporations for political contributions or other forms of patronage. One of the most difficult problems for corporate decision makers is knowing how to respond to such requests, and to what extent these requests represent a normal cost of doing business in such countries. It should be remembered that any payment involves a payor and payee, and that the payment is by no means always instigated by the payor.

The interdependencies created by international investment are inevitably going to involve countries in settling disputes involving multinational corporations. Corporations of convenience should be viewed as one set of actions with which governments will have to contend. Aside from international agreements, one way of handling this situation is for governments to decide whether they should allow such corporations to be established within their jurisdiction in the first place, and, if they do not allow them, to determine what the economic implications are likely to be. In the case of Canada, this will involve a much more explicit recognition of the existence of CDIA, and a closer relationship between government and business, and between the Deparment of External Affairs and the Department of Industry, Trade and Commerce.[26]

Electrohome in Malaysia

Between 1971 and 1973 five firms have actually invested in developing countries after undertaking CIDA-supported starter and feasibility studies. These firms are Electrohome Ltd. and Microsystems International Ltd. in Malaysia, Reliable Toy Co. Ltd. in Jamaica, and Monarch West and Peerless Wear in Brazil. One aim of CIDA is to promote industrial development in developing countries through the foreign operations of Canadian based firms — aid through investment is the rationale underlying this approach.

Electrohome Ltd. is a fully integrated Canadian owned firm operating in the electronics industry. CIDA financing assisted Electrohome in establishing a wholly owned subsidiary in Kuala Lumpur to produce electronic sub-assemblies which were previously purchased on an arms length basis from suppliers in the Far East. The firm felt that there were significant advantages to be gained from owning its own operation, one of which was an hourly wage rate about one-tenth of that in Canada. The Malaysian government provided considerable fiscal advantages to firms locating in Malaysia, for example, a five-year tax holiday for corporations which export 100% of their production, duty-free importation of equipment, and establishment of free-trade zones.

In essence, Electrohome's subsidiary in Malaysia acted as a manufacturing enclave, using local labour and certain inputs such as local utility services, and exporting all its output. From the country's point of view the company does bring benefits, but at the same time the arrangement can backfire politically with repercussions for the Canadian government. The fiscal advantages given to foreign companies are exactly the issues which local nationalists use when making foreign investment a political issue. This has been seen over and over again from the Zambian copper industry to the Central American banana industry. This is not to argue that CIDA should not encourage Canadian firms to invest abroad, but to stress that it must appreciate that the very situations which it is promoting may in future be used as issues to criticize the Canadian government.

There are a number of measures which can be employed to blunt such possible attacks. The form of the investment is important and the promotion of a joint venture with foreign capital may be viewed more favourably by a host country. Second, the developing country can be requested to state the conditions which are acceptable to it, especially whether planned divestment is to be undertaken in the future. Third, the Canadian government can provide investment insurance in all instances where investment results from CIDA initiatives.

SUMMARY OBSERVATIONS

These cases illustrate issues which have and will arise in connection with Canadian direct investment abroad. It is no longer adequate to treat CDIA as an issue that may go away, since there is increasing likelihood that as more firms invest abroad more issues will arise requiring some response on the part of the Canadian government.

In addition, the demand by developing countries for the establishment of a new economic order will undoubtedly have repercussions for government policy. This has already been manifest in the cooperation of resource-producing countries to enhance the returns from the production and sales of different kinds of natural resources. For example, producer country cartels have been organized with respect to bauxite, copper, bananas, and coffee. Finally, a response will be required to developments stemming from the GEP report on multinational corporations. Canada will have to decide what position to take with respect to the international monitoring of direct foreign investment. Two points need to be recognized. First, multinational corporations cannot operate separately from the political life of the host countries so that there will inevitably be some degree of political involvement. Second, even if home countries want to divorce themselves from the foreign operations of their companies, they will become drawn into issues, often as a direct result of host government initiatives.

The potential for conflict between the Canadian government and Canadian firms with investment abroad in developing countries is being increased by the apparent position taken by Canada at recent Commonwealth and United Nations meetings (September 1975). Canada is encouraging Canadian firms to increase their investments in the Third World, while at the same time sharing the host countries' concern over the exploitative activities of multinational enterprises. This may result in a situation where the governments of host countries may request the Canadian government to help modify the behaviour of Canadian multinationals in a way which may run counter to the initial support given by the Canadian government to these firms. Aside from the political implications of such activities, there is the more fundamental question of what is the appropriate nature of government/business relations.

NOTES

1. "International Development: A New Dimension for Canadian Business", address by Minister of Trade and Commerce to the Seminar on International Development, York University, Toronto, 6 November, 1967.

2. Speech by the Hon. A. Gillespie to the annual meeting of the Canadian Export Association, Ottawa, 29 October, 1974.

3. Webley, *Foreign Direct Investment in the United States: Opportunities and Impediments* (New York: British-North American Committee, September, 1974), p. 41.

4. Export Development Corporation Act, 1968-69, Ch. 39, S. 1, in *Revised Statutes of Canada 1970,* III, E-18 (Ottawa, 1970), pp. 2917-32.

5. Export Development Corporation, *EDC's Foreign Investment Guarantee Programme,* 1 February, 1978, p. 1.

6. *Ibid.*

7. Export Development Corporation, *Annual Report, 1976,* p. 30; *Annual Report, 1978,* pp. 8-11, 29-30.

8. EDC, *Annual Report, 1976,* p. 30.

9. See, T.H. Moran, "Transnational Strategies of Protection and Defense by Multinational Corporations: Spreading the Risk and Raising the Cost for Nationalization in Natural Resources", *International Organization,* Vol. 27, (Spring, 1973), pp. 273-87.

10. Canadian International Development Agency, *Canada and Development Co-operation,* Ottawa, 1976), p. 104.

11. *Ibid.*

12. *Public Relations Bulletin* issued by Information Division, Communications Branch, CIDA, Ottawa.

13. *Ibid.,* pp. 80-81, 109, CIDA, *Annual Review, 1977-78,* p. 25.

14. Notes for an address by Michel Dupuy at a business oriented seminar at Edmonton, 6 February, 1979, p. 5.

15. *Ibid.,* p. 10.

16. "A Citizen's Guide to the Herb Gray Report", *Canadian Forum* Vol. 51, (December, 1971), p. 71.

17. Canada, Senate, *Debates,* 8 December, 1970, p. 297.

18. Canada, House of Commons, *Debates,* 23 February, 1971, p. 3658.

19. For further details, see I.A. Litvak and C.J. Maule, "Nationalization in the Caribbean Bauxite Industry", *International Affairs,* Vol. 51, (January, 1975), pp. 43-59.

20. See *Multinational Corporations and U.S. Foreign Policy,* United States Senate, Subcommittee on Multinational Corporations of the Committee on Foreign Relations, 93rd Cong., March-April, 1973, Part I (Washington, 1973), p. 218.

21. *The Impact of Multinational Corporations on the Development Process and International Relations* (New York: United Nations Department of Economic and Social Affairs 1974), E/5500/Rev. 1 ST/ESA/6.

22. *Ibid.,* p. 47.

23. Barcelona Traction Case (Belgium vs. Spain) 1970, *International Legal Materials,* IX(2), International Court of Justice.

24. The Japanese government gives direction to Japanese firms investing abroad. See I.A. Litvak and C.J. Maule, "Japan's Overseas Investments", *Pacific Affairs,* Vol. 46, (Summer, 1973), 254-68.

25. *The Impact of Multinational Corporations,* p. 49.

26. In the case of the nationalization of Demba in Guyana, an interdepartmental commitee was set up to monitor negotiations. Its effectiveness was questionable, because of its ad hoc nature, and because of the distance between the corporate and government officials.

Chapter 6

Foreign Investment and Codes of Conduct

The issue of the control of the behaviour of international business activities has been a traditional focus for much of the policy debates over multinational enterprises. During the late 1960s and the early 1970s, attention was given to the implementation of regulations and legislation aimed at redressing perceived imbalances of power between multinational enterprises and host governments, and at ensuring that investors conformed to local policies and objectives for economic and social development. These concerns were reflected in efforts to screen proposed investments, to enforce local content requirements, and, in some countries, to compel the forcible divestiture of existing operations.

However, it has been increasingly recognized that this approach can be limited by the overall economic power of multinational enterprises, and by their ability to exploit disparities in legislative requirements between nations. Parent governments have expressed concern over the need to protect foreign direct investment against unilateral actions, and the damage to their foreign policies, which could result from cases of misconduct involving the overseas operations of domestic firms. These factors have led to efforts in recent years to establish basic ground rules for international investment, that is, to increase the social accountability of multinational enterprises and to censor or proscribe questionable behaviour.

Perhaps the most visible form of social efforts to influence the foreign operations of companies has been the presentation of proxy resolutions at annual stockholders' meetings by public interest activists. For instance, during 1979, from a total of 130 shareholder resolutions presented at annual meetings for American corporations, 34 called upon managers to cease commercial operations in the Republic of South Africa and 14 demanded a cessation of trade with other repressive governments.[1] In Canada, similar resolutions, which are aimed at changing the locations in which foreign direct investment is placed, have been presented at the annual meetings of companies such as Falconbridge and Noranda Mines.

In some cases, external interest groups have made protests over relatively small investments. For example, in 1977, Canadian Superior Oil joined a consortium with a 22.5% interest in a $5 million programme of exploration and evaluation of copper properties at Quebrada Blanca in Chile. At the company's 1978 annual meeting, representatives from three Canadian church organizations claimed that even though the project was extremely high-risk in nature, it could have a payoff of $500 million. They suggested that Canadian Superior withdraw from the study, since the development of any deposits would tend to strengthen the rule of the Chilean junta. The proposal was rejected.

As a rule, multinational enterprises have sought to avoid conflicts and to retain a low public profile in the conduct of business operations. From the perspective of the corporation, the extent to which social responsibility issues should be taken into account during the formulation of business plans can represent a major dilemma. Mr. A.R. Nielson, the President and Chief Executive Officer of Canadian Superior, indicated that the firm had to deal with both left and right wing governments.

> If we restricted our activities to countries that share our political and business beliefs we would be locked out of the majority of countries of the world.
>
> We don't think that the postponement of our work there would have any effect on the political conditions or that it would help the people. We do not agree with the Government's policies but abandoning our interests there would accomplish absolutely nothing.[2]

From the perspective of the external interest groups, the adverse publicity engendered by these incidents can serve as a deterrent against corporate policies which they oppose; but given the tendency for most shareholder resolutions to fail, the effectiveness of the strategy is open to question.

Contemporary efforts to control or guide the behaviour of international investors have largely centred upon the use of codes of conduct. The concept of a code is best characterized as ambiguous, with a lack of any specific legal meaning or scope. However, it can be described as a set of recommendations or rules which may be mandatory or voluntary in nature, and which are addressed to governments, corporations or individuals. Consequently, a code constitutes a compilation of existing legislation and regulations which must be adhered to at all times; or it may be an instrument of moral suasion with advice which should be followed according to experience and the circumstances of any given situation.[3]

Codes of conduct can be segmented into four categories based on their origin:

(1) *Corporate* — adopted voluntarily by the international investor.

(2) *National* — introduced by a government for the domestic operations

of foreign companies, or the foreign subsidiaries of domestic corporations.

(3) *Regional* — adopted by organizations representing groupings of countries for implementation by multinational firms and member states.

(4) *International* — adopted by international organizations for implementation by all countries and firms. An objective of some governments, this option is currently only a speculative option.

The remainder of this chapter is devoted to an analysis of those codes of conduct which may influence the activities of Canadian direct investment abroad. Consideration is first given to the phenomena of corporate codes, as illustrated by the codes of conduct adopted by Inco and Massey-Ferguson, and then to the use of a regional instrument, such as the guidelines adopted by the Organization for Economic Cooperation and Development. Finally, Canadian government policies on the behaviour of inward investment and the foreign operations of state owned companies, as well as trade with South Africa and the Arab nations, will be highlighted.

CORPORATE CODES

Initial efforts to establish general standards of international business behaviour tended to come from those companies and organizations which operate on a multinational basis. As early as 1952, the United States Council of the International Chamber of Commerce developed a set of voluntary guidelines for foreign investors and submitted them to the International Chamber of Commerce (ICC). However, after two years of discussions, the ICC decided to abandon this proposal because of the complexity of creating common standards for a diversity of industries and firms, and because many businessmen feared that host countries might perceive the guidelines as a set of rules to be used even in cases for which they would be inappropriate.[4]

The proliferation of legislation and regulations affecting foreign direct investment, at a national level during the late 1960s, compelled the ICC to adopt a set of guidelines for international investment which were recommended to member firms and organizations. The rules reflect the traditional concerns of businessmen for facilitating foreign investment activities and for the minimization of potential restrictions on international corporate practices. A voluntary effort at self-regulation by multinational enterprises could limit the amount of conflict with nation states and local interest groups. The guidelines consequently attempted to set out the roles and responsibilities of corporations, as well as parent and host governments.

In particular, the guidelines recommended that:

(1) Host governments should provide equal treatment for foreign and domestic enterprises. Prior consultation between companies and governments, as well as pre-investment contractual arrangements, should be encouraged.

(2) Multinational enterprises should allow the use of joint ventures and local equity participation in less developed countries, but these arrangements should be established through free negotiations and without compulsory local ownership requirements.

(3) No protectionist restrictions of imports and exports of goods, or of capital outflows, should be allowed, save in cases where there are serious balance of payments problems. Corporations should take into account the impact which their policies could have upon a host country's balance of payments.

(4) Local competition laws should be respected but these laws should not be applied extraterritorially by either home or host nations.

(5) Investment disputes should be resolved through international arbitration when necessary, and property rights should be respected under the existing international legal conventions. Host countries should respect the provisions of pre-investment contractual arrangements, and provide just and expedient repayment when expropriations do occur.[5]

A similar privately initiated set of voluntary guidelines, the *Pacific Basin Charter,* was adopted in 1972 by the Pacific Basin Economic Council. The Council is an association including more than 400 corporate officials from Canada, the United States, New Zealand, Australia, and Japan. The United States Chamber of Commerce, the Canadian Chamber of Commerce, and the British Chamber of Commerce have also adopted similar codes of ethics for members.

The promulgation of corporate codes of conduct became particularly prominent during the late 1970s, a trend which can be traced to a policy decision made by the United States Securities and Exchange Commission (SEC). Following its 1975 investigation of Gulf Oil and United Brands for bribery and illegal political contributions, the SEC recognized that it lacked the manpower to examine the possible business improprieties of the more than 9,000 publicly listed companies which came under its jurisdiction. Consequently, the SEC developed a disclosure programme under which firms could report voluntarily any questionable or illegal accounting practices and foreign payments. Participation in the programme by a corporation would improve, but not necessarily guarantee, the probability that the SEC would fail to take legal action against it.[6]

When there are grounds to believe that material facts exist which should be disclosed, a firm authorizes a detailed investigation of the incidents by individuals who were not involved in the activities. This investigation has normally been conducted by a special committee of the company's board of directors, comprised solely of non-management directors, who are assisted by independent legal counsel and accountants. The investigation must cover the preceding five years at the very least, and must secure detailed information on every questionable payment or practice. The findings are reported to the board which must issue appropriate policies to terminate the questionable activities, and to create adequate control and monitoring procedures to ensure that they are not repeated. A final report on the investigation is then filed with the SEC on Form 8-K.[7]

Since the costs of making a disclosure were significantly less than those of litigation, more than 360 companies filed reports by March 1977, including several Canadian corporations which were listed on the New York Stock Exchange.[8] The 8-K reports of two Canadian enterprises, Inco and Massey-Ferguson, are reprinted in Appendix B and may be utilized as case illustrations of the corporate response to increasing social censorship.

Both firms acknowledged that they had provided *facilitating payments* to government functionaries in order to secure documents and permits which these officials legally were supposed to issue. The payments had been made in countries where they were considered a customary practice, even if it was illegal in nature. In the case of Inco, the total value of the payments over a six year period amounted to $240,000 U.S., and each disbursement normally did not exceed $100 U.S. ESB, an Inco subsidiary, made payments totalling $130,000 U.S. to government officials as a means of securing reductions in duty and tax obligations, commercial information, or permits. Massey-Ferguson admitted to giving $12,000 U.S. to an official who could influence $2.3 million U.S. worth of government contracts with one of its subsidiaries. The company paid $2.4 million U.S. in commissions to three agents for affecting sales; it is probable that some of the monies were used to bribe officials.

To some degree, both firms had engaged in the falsification of records. Inco noted that some of the questionable payments had been inadequately documented, or inappropriately charged in its books. Three foreign subsidiaries of ESB maintained off-book cash accounts, worth a maximum of $140,000 U.S. to make questionable payments. On several occasions, Massey-Ferguson overbilled and underbilled different subsidiaries as a means of transferring funds, thereby evading foreign exchange controls, local content requirements, or tax and banking regulations.

By remitting commissions and service fees through numbered bank accounts or to associates in third countries, both companies enabled some clients to potentially evade tax and exchange control regulations. Massey-Ferguson overbilled certain distributors $30.5 million U.S.

during a five year period, and subsequently provided them with rebates, normally via a third country. Since the practice involves the distortion of the profit and sales statistics of different subsidiaries, it represented a form of profit skimming and defrauding of stockholders' interests in the company.

In fairness, it should be observed that the monies affected by these activities were insignificant relative to total corporate revenues. In both cases, questionable practices were related to less than 1% of sales, and there was a tendency for senior managers to be unaware of their existence. In the case of Inco, a significant proportion of these practices were carried out by ESB, a subsidiary which was acquired during the period under investigation. It could be legitimately argued that a failure to quickly harmonize ESB's policies with those of the parent company was a contributing factor to the use of questionable practices.

Like other corporations participating in the SEC disclosure programme, Inco and Massey-Ferguson adopted codes of ethics as a means of eliminating inappropriate behaviour. The basic principles of these guidelines can be summarized as follows:

(1) Employees should act in accordance with the laws of host countries; the use of corporate assets, liabilities and property for illegal purposes is forbidden.

(2) When political contributions are made, the practice should conform to the laws and customs of host countries, and the payments should be small enough to avoid the impression that special treatment is being sought.

(3) Although the use of bribery and kickbacks will be banned, companies will continue to make *facilitating payments* when they are in accordance with local customs, and are necessary to avoid the obstruction of normal commercial operations.

(4) Cash funds, bank accounts, and assets shall not be kept outside of a company's regular accounting and financial records; all transactions with clients will be recorded accurately and shall not be obscured.

(5) The use of overbilling practices, false invoicing or misleading documentation will be terminated. Rebates will not be made if illicit purposes or legal liability are involved.

(6) Clients will be paid via third countries only when there is written authorization for the remission, common ownership between the client and the recipient, and no legal liability.

(7) A monitoring procedure will be established in order to ensure that corporate executives are aware of the guidelines and adhere to them.

Corporate codes of conduct do not merely represent a public affairs manoeuvre to improve company image. Rather, they constitute a serious effort by firms to neutralize some of the sources of conflict with nation-states and local interest groups, and in some enterprises they have been rigorously enforced.[9] Guidelines can be particularly useful to those firms which have limited experience with foreign investments, and can indicate some of the problem areas which should be avoided.[10]

However, the impact and utility of corporate codes should not be overestimated. Some governments and interest groups have been inclined to see in the very promulgation of guidelines a confirmation of prior suspicions of corporate misconduct; therefore, company codes cannot be expected to mollify external critics and opponents. Since the codes have been unilaterally adopted and are self-regulatory in nature, their role as a control mechanism is widely distrusted. The effectiveness of implementation of codes has been largely contingent upon the degree of moral leadership and formal authority exercised by senior executives. In addition, the codes tend to be phrased in such a general manner that they have a limited value to managers as guides for decision-making in specific situations.

Corporate codes tend to approach questionable behaviour from a narrow perspective, and focus upon the prevention of actions which could lead to legal sanctions being quickly imposed upon the protection of property rights. The codes normally fail to deal with a broad range of issues of concern to external parties such as anti-competitive and pricing practices, influence upon labour relations and social norms, or the disclosure of information and technical knowledge. Moreover, while company codes attempt to ensure that the laws of host countries are adhered to, they usually do not take adequate account of the increasing efforts of some governments and interest groups to apply extraterritorially those standards of behaviour which are viewed as acceptable in parent nations. Finally, reflecting the traditional attitudes of businessmen, these codes do not concede as legitimate any efforts to limit their freedoms in the marketplace. These other concerns have been significant factors in the establishment of guidelines for multinational enterprises at the national and regional levels.

THE OECD GUIDELINES

Approximately 75% of Canadian direct investment abroad has been placed in the industrialized nations which dominate the Organization for Economic Cooperation and Development (OECD). In 1974, various committees and ad hoc working groups at the OECD began to investigate the policy implications of multinational enterprise activities and to formulate standards of corporate behaviour. In 1975, these efforts were consolidated under a Committee for International Investment and Multinational Enterprises, which produced a code of conduct adopted by the member states in June, 1976. These guidelines represent the first time that a set of policy commitments based upon a codification of the mutual responsibilities of governments and international firms has been adopted by those countries accounting for the bulk of global trade and investment. In order to understand the substance and implications of this agreement, it is necessary to review those factors which led to its development.

When the OECD was established in 1960, its objectives included that of contributing

> to the expansion of World Trade on a multi-lateral and non-discriminatory basis, in conformity with international obligations.[11]

As part of this mandate, during 1961, the OECD adopted a code for the liberalization of capital movements, which called upon member states to handle the investment of foreign and domestic enterprise in the same manner and not to restrict the international transfer of assets and profits. In 1967, a draft Convention for the Protection of Foreign Holdings was published, but not formally accepted, which recommended that countries should provide protection and security to foreign investments and

> in no way hamper their management, their maintenance, their utilization, their enjoyment, . . . by any unjustified or discriminatory measures.[12]

The developed nations historically have viewed the multinational enterprise as a predominantly beneficial mechanism for economic development. Maintaining the existence of liberal investment climates and safeguarding the property rights of enterprises have been their primary concerns, particularly of the government of the United States. This perspective is reflected in the OECD code which declares that:

> The common aim of the Member countries is to encourage the positive contributions which multinational enterprises can make to economic and social progress and to minimize the difficulties to which their various operations may give rise . . .[13]

In contrast, the developing countries tend to treat the multinational enterprise with marked distrust, as a real threat to their economic and political sovereignty, due to its ability to determine prices or to influence trade balances, labour conditions, and social norms. This viewpoint is compounded by a widespread belief that the multinational enterprise itself does not represent a legitimate economic entity, but merely serves as an extension of a dominating and exploitive market system, which reserves the primary benefits of foreign investments to the industrialized nations.[14] Thus, by the late 1960s, numerous less developed countries were confronted with the paradox of needing foreign investment for economic development, while also wanting to strengthen their control over multinational business activities, a situation which resulted in a proliferation of regional and national laws aimed at redressing perceived balances of power.[15]

From the perspective of the developed countries, particularly the United States, there was a serious risk that these efforts to restrict foreign investments would be replicated in international bodies. In 1972, the United Nations Economic and Social Council asked for the establishment of a *Group of Eminent Persons* to study the impact of the multinational corporation on economic development and international relations. In turn, the group recommended that a commission on multinational enterprises and a Centre on Transnational Corporations be established. The group also recommended that a code of conduct be developed comprising

> . . . a consistent set of recommendations which are gradually evolved and which may be revised as experience or circumstances require. Although they are not compulsory in nature, they act as an instrument of moral persusaion, strengthened by the authority of international organization and the support of public opinion.[16]

The commission, which was established in 1974, has given priority to the development of a code of conduct as one method of regulating international business activities, and as a means of providing a greater degree of standardization across disparate national and regional legislation, thereby reducing jurisdictional disputes.[17] The developing countries have called for a code which would focus on specific issues and curtail the market freedoms exercised by multinational enterprises, and which would be legally binding upon all parties with penalties for non-compliance. The industrialized nations have insisted that a binding code would prove impractical for implementation, and that.guidelines should be developed which would be based on "general and equitable principles."[18]

At the present time, there are no established precedents in international law for a supra-national legal instrument which would be binding upon all nations automatically. Resolutions and conventions passed through international organizations, such as the United Nations, cannot be binding upon member states without their consent. However, there was a serious possibility that less developed countries would use their voting power to pass a restrictive model code through the General Assembly, and then incorporate its provision in national legislation.

From the perspectives of the industrialized countries, developing a separate code of conduct through the OECD could serve as one means of taking immediate action to modify multinational enterprise behaviour and thereby reduce pressure for major restrictions on multinational enterprise activities. As the product of a relatively favourable forum, an OECD code could be used as a basic bargaining position in subsequent negotiations with less developed countries for the development of a more widely acceptable set of rules.

The OECD guidelines contain the following nine basic principles which should be adhered to by international investors:

(1) The general policy objectives of both host and parent countries should be taken into account when corporate decisions are made.

(2) Special recognition should be given to the objectives and priorities of host and parent nations in terms of factors relating to economic and social progress.

(3) Companies should be prepared not only to fulfill legal requirements for the disclosure of data on their financial and operating activities, but also to provide any supplemental information relevant to the assessment of any potential impact upon domestic policies.

(4) International investors should cooperate with and support local social and business interests.

(5) Within the constraints imposed by the needs for product specialization and for the harmonization of corporate commercial operations, subsidiaries and affiliates should have the autonomy necessary for the development and exploitation of competitive advantages in local and export markets.

(6) Within the context of local legislative requirements, hiring and promotion practices in each country should be based on the principle of individual merit and should not discriminate against nationalities.

(7) Foreign investors should not offer bribes or questionable payments to government officials and public representatives, either directly or indirectly.

(8) Unless permitted under national law, political contributions should not be made.

(9) Investors should avoid any questionable involvement in local politics.

The OECD code then focusses on six subject areas:

(1) Disclosure of information.

(2) Competition policy.

(3) Balance of payments and monetary policies.

(4) Transfer pricing and taxation.

(5) Employee rights

(6) Access to technology. (See Appendix C)

As a set of voluntary rules for multinational enterprises, the OECD guidelines represent a major inter-governmental accord about the sort of activities which constitute acceptable business behaviour, as well as a significant effort to achieve a degree of harmonization and collaboration among the industrialized states for the treatment of international investments.

While imposing *de facto* obligations on business firms, the OECD guidelines also place specific responsibilities on host governments. Under the national treatment proviso, signatories agreed that a long-term objective should be to give similar treatment to foreign and domestic enterprises. Restrictions on the sectors in which foreign investment is allowed, and the grounds for formal discrimination on the basis of corporate nationality, must be publicly disclosed. Member states agreed to consult on the use of investment incentives and disincentives, and to respect provisions of international laws relating to corporations such as conventions on intellectual property rights. From a corporate perspective, these agreements clarify the rules for international investment, thereby reducing the risk of punititve governmental actions, such as expropriation without compensation.

Criticisms of current transnational codes of conduct in general, and of the OECD guidelines in particular, have centred primarily upon the use of a nonbinding approach. It has been contended that multinational enterprises will be compelled to modify noticeably their behaviour only if sanctions and penalties can be legally imposed and enforced by national or international institutions.[19] While past examples of corporate activities could be cited readily in support of this perspective, it should be noted that adherence to the codes will not be quite as voluntary as may seem to be evident initially, and that their promulgation was meant to have a significant impact upon transnational business operations.

Even though multinational enterprises have not formally agreed to follow the principles of the guidelines, having been involved in their formulation and having offered numerous proposals which were subsequently adopted by the participating governments, a failure to honour the principles of the code would be widely interpreted as inconsistent and unconscionable behaviour on the part of transnational firms.[20] Since the guidelines have been endorsed by all of the major developed countries as standards of good conduct for both national and international enterprise, clear identification at variance with the rules would subject a company to extremely poor public relations at the very least.

Indeed, the very fact that the members of the OECD have reached a consensus on a set of standards and recommend them to multinational enterprises alters the purely voluntary aspect of the declaration, since it provides the guidelines with a significant moral and practical political influence upon the actions of enterprises and parent or host governments.[21] The use of general or nonbinding agreements has been frequent in international relations. Moreover, once governments do reach mutual understandings, even for nonbinding arrangements, the participants can be expected to inquire into and insist upon each other's actual execution of their provisions even if these were previously viewed as subject to discretionary action or reserved for domestic jurisdiction.

. . .By entering into an international pact with other states, a party may be presumed to have agreed that the matters covered are no longer exclusively its concern. When other parties make representations or offer criticism about conduct at variance with the undertakings in the agreement, the idea of a commitment is reinforced, even if it is labelled as political or moral. . . . As long as they do last, even nonbinding agreements can be authoritative and controlling for the parties. There is no *a priori* reason to assume that the undertakings are illusory because they are not legal. . . .[22]

The OECD Guidelines place particular stress on the need for national governments to be provided with full information on multinational enterprise activities and, as shown in Appendix C, advise transnationals not only to disclose information on local enterprises to host states, but also to supply data on global operations to permit the evaluation of issues such as transfer pricing and the autonomy of subsidiaries. Moreover, an OECD Committee on International Investment and Multinational Enterprises has served since 1976 as a forum for member countries to exchange views on the principles of the code problems encountered in its application. When conflicting demands do arise, the affected governments are expected to cooperate in good faith with a view to resolving such problems, either within the committee, or through other mutually acceptable arrangements.

Commercial and labour organizations are periodically invited to discuss the principles of the guidelines through advisory committees to the OECD. Multinational enterprises may be requested to offer opinions on the actual application of the code although they may not initiate consultations. Particular incidents may be used to illustrate the problems involved in broad issue areas as a means of clarifying the guidelines and their intended effects; but the committee has been enjoined against the investigation of any specific incident or the assessment of the conduct of individual enterprises. However, this proviso has not precluded particular actions of some multinational enterprises from being drawn to the OECD's attention. During 1976 and 1977, trade unions presented incidents to the committee in which transnational firms were alleged to have infringed the code. One of these incidents was raised directly by the Belgian government.[23]

In 1979, the OECD Council at ministerial level reviewed the first three years of the guidelines based on a report of the OECD Committee on International Investment and Multinational Enterprises. The ministers felt that the 1976 instruments had been effective in contributing to a favourable investment climate, and in producing a sound basis for cooperation between governments, multinational enterprises and employees. The review noted, in particular, a revision made in 1979 to provisions relating to employment and industrial relations. The revision dealt with the use made by a firm to transfer employees and production from one plant to another, in order to enhance the firm's negotiating position in labour disputes. The Canadian government was noted as having been active in disseminating the 1976 guidelines to government departments and to business, and as having held discussions with the business and labour communities in Canada on the application of the 1976 instruments.[24]

Canada's concurrence in OECD guidelines in June, 1976 can be attributed to the policies of federal and provincial governments toward inward, rather than outward, investment flows. At that time, the Minister for External Affairs noted that imported capital had been extensively relied upon for Canadian industrial development, and, consequently, that high levels of foreign ownership had been attained which were unparalleled among the OECD nations. While acknowledging that foreign investment "has undoubtedly conferred economic benefits on Canada", the minister observed that, since the 1960s, the orientation of domestic public policy had shifted towards improving the responsiveness of foreign controlled companies to Canadian needs, and towards strengthening the role of Canadian owned enterprises.[25]

From the perspective of the federal government, the nonbinding nature of the code provided host countries with flexibility for their interpretations. But, in particular,

> . . . We would note that the promulgation of these Guidelines in no way infringes on the right of governments to prescribe, in the interests of achieving national economic and social goals, the conditions under which multinational enterprises may operate in their jurisdiction.[26]

Although Canada wanted more inward investment and adhered to the general concept of *national treatment*, both federal and provincial administrations reserved the right to take special measures affecting foreign investors which they felt were appropriate for the protection of domestic interests.

Canadian exceptions to the *national treatment* clause can be segmented into three broad areas: (1) differential treatment of investment proposals by domestic or foreign parties; (2) varying rights to official aid and subsidies, as well as to government contracts; and (3) distinctions in tax obligations.[27]

Investment Controls

Under the provisions of the 1974 Foreign Investment Review Act, the federal government has the authority to screen and approve those investment proposals which are made by non-Canadian citizens, foreign controlled enterprises or foreign governments, and non-resident Canadians. The act applies to both acquisitions of Canadian controlled firms and the establishment of new businesses in Canada. Proposals by foreign controlled firms already located in Canada are also subject to review if they involve the establishment of new businesses which are unrelated to their existing operations. Exemptions from the screening process occur when an enterprise being acquired does not have gross assets worth more than $250,000 or revenues greater than $3 million, or if it is related to the firm making the acquisition.

Those parties whose proposals fall within the provisions of the act must demonstrate that their investments will provide *significant benefit* to Canada. Assessments are made on the basis of five criteria:

(1) the impact on economic activity, including factors such as employment, the processing of Canadian resources, and the development of exports;

(2) the degree and significance of Canadian participation in ownership and management, as well as the acquiescence of the existing owners in takeover cases;

(3) the effect on productivity, efficiency, and technological development;

(4) the effect on competition; and

(5) the compatibility with national and provincial industrial and economic policies.[28]

Although the practice does not strictly fall within the concept of *national treatment,* Canada, like other members of the OECD, has designated some sectors to be of strategic economic or cultural significance. The federal government restricts the right of entry by foreign investors into banking and other financial institutions, broadcasting, insurance, publishing, and certain aspects of resource development, such as uranium mining and refining. Similarly, the Quebec government regulates foreign involvement in trust companies. At the federal and provincial levels there are laws and regulations which stipulate that the chairman and a majority of the board of directors, in both Canadian and foreign controlled companies, be Canadians.

Right to Aid and Contracts

This category refers to differential treatment accorded to domestic and foreign enterprises by governments in their employment, regional and industrial incentive programmes, or in their selection of contractors. For example, under federal regulations, grants for the exploration of minerals in northern Canada are limited to Canadian citizens and to corporations which are listed on Canadian stock exchanges or are at least 50% Canadian owned; while on a provincial level, Alberta restricts loans or loan guarantees issued by the Alberta Agricultural Development Corporation to Canadian residents and to companies which are incorporated in Canada, and do not have more than 20% foreign ownership.

The exceptions in this category, which have been declared by the Canadian government, significantly understate the amount of differential treatment which actually occurs, a phenomenon which is equally true of other OECD countries. For example, they do not take into account administrative practices which discriminate on the basis of business nationality. Some federal and provincial government purchase programmes deliberately favour contract bids from domestically controlled firms as part of *buy Canadian* policies, and Canadian research and development schemes are primarily oriented towards the development of Canadian-owned enterprises.[29]

Tax Obligations

As in the cases of Sweden and Australia. Canadian governments deny certain tax deductions and incentives to foreign companies or charge them special duties for certain transactions. Under the Income Tax Act, non-Canadian corporations are not entitled to tax-free provisions for roll-overs of assets, and cannot qualify as special status enterprises, such as investment or mortgage investment corporations. The province of Ontario imposes transfer taxes on acquisitions of land by non-residents at a rate of 20% of the value at the time of sale; in contrast, residents only pay 0.3% on the first $35,000 of sales and 0.6% on the balance. Quebec also charges duties on land transfers to non-resident persons.

CANADIAN ATTITUDES TOWARDS INWARD INVESTMENT

It was previously observed that Canadian policy has been oriented towards inward flows of foreign investment. Since the country is relatively unique in terms of the extensive role of foreign controlled firms in certain sectors of the domestic economy, it is not surprising that Canadian government policies towards inward investment largely antedate those of other industrialized nations. Nevertheless, there has traditionally been a receptive attitude towards foreign investors. Until 1974, there was no machinery for monitoring and checking inward flows of investments. During the last 15 years, Canadian governments have sought to harmonize the behaviour and activities of foreign investors with domestic policies and interests.

Early in 1966, the Minister for Trade and Commerce, the Honourable Robert Winters, wrote to the chief executives of 3,500 foreign companies operating in Canada, and stressed the need for their enterprises to identify with Canadian interests and to participate in Canadian economic development. In particular, 12 guiding principles for good corporate citizenship were outlined, and are reprinted in Appendix D. These guidelines can be summarized as follows:

(1) Foreign companies should encourage the growth and development of their Canadian subsidiaries in accordance with federal government industrial policies. Efforts should be made to maximize the amount of purchasing from Canadian sources, exporting, and

secondary manufacturing carried out by their Canadian operations.

(2) Within the constraints imposed by the efficient allocation of corporate resources, Canadian subsidiaries should become vertically integrated entities with complete responsibility for at least one product line, and should retain an indigenous capability for research and product development.

(3) Earnings and profits derived from Canadian subsidiaries should be reinvested domestically, and not be repatriated or used to expand operations in other countries.

(4) Foreign corporations should encourage Canadian equity participation, and should use Canadian citizens as managers and directors, in order to ensure a sensitivity to local conditions in planning and product development, as well as to provide an impact by Canadians upon the formulation of policies.

(5) Companies should periodically publish information on the financial conditions and operations of their Canadian subsidiaries, rather than merely consolidate relevant data into statements of total corporate performance.

(6) As a means of strengthening their ties to local communities, foreign firms should provide support to Canadian cultural and charitable institutions.

The Winters guidelines were non-binding in nature, although several provisions have subsequently become part of Canadian laws and regulations, such as Canadian citizens forming a majority of directors in federally incorporated companies. To a very real extent, the Winters guidelines represent an early version of the criteria used by FIRA after 1974 to screen proposals made by foreigners for investments in Canada.

These guidelines were revised and expanded in 1975 by the minister responsible for FIRA, the Hon. Allistair Gillespie (Appendix D). The 1975 code contains all of the provisions of the Winters guidelines, and adds, the following two principles:

(1) Foreign companies should resist any direct or indirect pressure from other governments to act in a contrary manner to the objectives and programmes of the Canadian government.

(2) Foreign firms should ensure that access to foreign resources and information is not restricted.

The primary difference between the Winters and the Gillespie guidelines is the use of more forceful language in the latter code to define the benefits which foreign firms are expected to provide and the actions which should be avoided. This shift in emphasis can be attributed to the increased nationalist sentiments and distrust of multinational enterprises which occurred over the intervening time period.

Specific Canadian guideline type policies on the behaviour of

Canadian direct investment abroad have emerged in connection with the role of state owned enterprises in international business, and on trade policy with South Africa. It is to these that attention will now be addressed.

CROWN CORPORATIONS

Paralleling the expansion of Canadian direct investment abroad by firms in the private sector, there has been a growth in the foreign operations of state enterprises, in particular, those of Crown corporations. It is estimated that total revenues earned by federal and provincial Crown corporations approximate 10% of Canada's gross national product.[30] For the sake of clarity, a federal Crown corporation is a wholly owned government enterprise which is ultimately accountable through a minister to parliament for the conduct of its affairs, and which has been designated as an official agent of the Crown under Part VIII of the 1951 Financial Administration Act. This type of organization does not include those corporations in which there is mixed ownership, or wholly owned government firms, such as DeHavilland Aircraft, which have not been designated as Crown agents.[31]

As of 1979, there were approximately 176 federal Crown corporations, many of which operated on a commercial or quasi-commercial basis such as Air Canada, the Canadian Broadcasting Corporation and Canadian National Railways. During the 1970s, these companies were not required to disclose their foreign holdings, and as a consequence, publicly accessible information severely understates the amount of Canadian direct investment abroad emanating from this source. Canadian National Railways alone has established approximately 100 subsidiaries outside Canada.

Those Crown corporations which operate on a commercial or quasi-commercial basis traditionally have been relatively independent of direct regulation. Controls have been minimal in order to avoid political interference which might jeopardize the ability of firms to compete without substantial government support, and to attract businessmen into state controlled enterprises. However, a need for guidelines for the international commercial activities of Crown corporations and government controlled corporations became apparent following two major scandals involving Polysar Ltd. and Atomic Energy of Canada Ltd. (AECL).

Polysar was established during the Second World War for the development of synthetic rubber. It was able to maintain a large amount of independence from the government throughout the 1950s and 1960s due to a high profit rate, which minimized the need for monetary support. In 1972, Polysar was sold to the Canada Development Corporation (CDC), a mixed enterprise which was 66% government owned.

During the period of 1970 to 1976, Polysar's Swiss subsisidiary, Polysar International S.A. (PISA), engaged in several questionable invoicing and payment practices. Subsequent investigations determined that 95% of PISA'a sales were conducted in an orderly and regular manner, and that only 13 direct customers and 14 distributors benefited from the actions.[32]

PISA supplied quantity discounts to several clients, a legitimate business practice *per se*. However, these monies were not paid directly to customers, but were channelled through numbered Swiss bank accounts. As a consequence, PISA's management did not know who the actual recipients were. Volume rebates were occasionally made, not to the purchasers, but to their foreign affiliates instead. In several cases, inflated purchase prices were charged to and paid by firms; rebates were provided to their foreign affiliates through numbered Swiss bank accounts. Some commissions of 15% of sales were paid to the subsidiaries of the actual distributors. In several other instances, while official commissions were provided to distributors, confidential marketing allowances were paid to associates in their parent countries for unspecified reasons.

It was alleged that the primary objectives of these actions included both evasion of foreign exchange control regulations and tax evasion on the part of PISA's clients by tranferrring funds to lower tax or tax-free domiciles. The manipulation of corporate accounts by mis-stating the value of sales and commissions constituted a form of profit-skimming, and therefore represented a defrauding of the Canadian government's equity interest in Polysar. It was subsequently charged that bribery may have been involved, but this claim was never proven.

The second scandal involved Atomic Energy of Canada Ltd. (AECL), a firm which originally evolved from the participation of the National Research Council and the Department of National Defence in the Manhattan Project. In 1953, the enterprise was incorporated as a Crown corporation responsible for nuclear energy research and its application for peaceful purposes, and for the management of the nuclear reactor at Chalk River. In 1968, AECL developed the CANDU reactor to the point that it became a commercially viable alternative to American fast breeder reactors as a safer and more efficient producer of energy; AECL also became major supplier of heavy water. During the period of 1970 to 1976, AECL came under intense pressure to sell CANDU reactors abroad. Foreign sales would indicate international acceptance of the economics and technology of the reactor, and would serve as the basis for the development of a high technology industry in Canada.

In its international attempts to sell the CANDU reactor, AECL became embroiled in a complex series of issues involving financial ineptitude, waste of public monies, and the use of questionable (if not illegal) business practices such as bribery.[33]

As a response to the AECL and Polysar incidents, during December, 1976, the Canadian government promulgated a code of conduct for the international commercial practices of Crown corporations. In announcing the guidelines, the President of the Treasury Board, the Hon. Robert Andras, acknowledged that a dichotomy had emerged between the goals of foreign trade promotion and the maintenance of publicly acceptable standards of behaviour. Problems had been encountered in that grey area in which fell

> ... the practices about which people who consider themselves to be of equal integrity can make differing judgements, practices whose ethical quality can be perceived differently in different societies, and even within the same society at different stages of its development.[34]

However, 25% of jobs and 56% of production in Canada were related to export trade alone, international business was a crucial matter for the country, and attention must be focussed upon immoral acts "which might jeopardize our trading activity or damage our external and trade relations."[35]

The guidelines, which are reproduced in Appendix E, contain the following provisions:

(1) Crown corporations are forbidden to take any actions in Canada which contravene Canadian laws, or to violate the laws of host countries in which they have commercial activities. Where conflicts of standards arise, Canadian law shall take precedence; that is, when there is any ambiguity about the propriety of any given act, Canadian legal and moral norms shall be extraterritorially applied.

(2) Employees of Crown corporations are prohibited from using or accepting bribes, as well as from engaging in influence peddling.

(3) Agents may only be utilized if there are written contracts which delineate the conditions of their employment, and if their operations are not illegal in those countries in which they are carried out.

(4) Boards of Directors of Crown corporations must establish written procedures for the approval of agency contracts, and must authorize any exemptions.

(5) The identities of any agents and the aggregate amount of payments to agencies per year must be disclosed by Crown corporations, effective with their 1978 annual reports.

The guidelines are not legally binding, although the possibility of enacting enforcement legislation was indicated at the time of their publication. The Treasury Board has the responsibility for ensuring that the affected enterprises adhere to the code, but to date, no review mechanisms have been established.

The guidelines are not only meant to apply to Crown corporations but also to mixed enterprises, such as the Canada Development Corporation and Panarctic Oils, and to wholly owned government enterprises which have not been made Crown corporations, such as Canadair and DeHavilland Aircraft. Similarly, the Ministry for External Affairs and the Ministry of Industry, Trade and Commerce were instructed to ensure that departmental procedures and practices conformed to the code. In particular, while trade commissioners and foreign services officers.

> . . . must do all they can to inform Canadian businessmen of all the factors that could influence their sales prospects, they must limit their assistance to providing information of a general and factual nature, and must under no circumstances counsel or advise the businessmen to engage in any corrupt or illegal practice.[36]

The guidelines have encountered extensive, and often derisive, criticism from businessmen and public servants. The government's contention that there are fundamental principles which should be adhered to in the use of questionable payments has been characterized as a naive approach to the conduct of commercial affairs in other countries. The vagueness of the code effectively limits its use in making decisions.

Moreover, the guidelines created a dilemma for Canadian foreign service officers in terms of the type of advice which they should provide to clients. For example, in 1978, DeHavilland Aircraft attempted to sell Dash 7s to the Indonesian government by utilizing their agent, but lost the contract. The firm was informed that their agent was out of favour, and another individual was suggested. The second agent tended to use bribes in his work, whereas the first did not. Does a Canadian commercial officer advise the company to utilize the second agent because he is successful, even though he frequently resorts to bribes, or is the first agent recommended with a concomitant probability of failure? The available evidence would suggest that Canadian officials have attempted to provide their clients with details on the implications of such alternatives, and let the affected companies make their own selections.

Further restrictions on the foreign operations of Crown corporations have become evident since the introduction of a Crown Corporations Act into parliament in late 1979. The bill contains provisions which would prohibit the foreign subsidiaries of Crown corporations from conducting any types of commercial activities which their parent firms have not been mandated to carry out within Canada. Where a dichotomy exists between these operations and the objectives set forth in enabling legislation or government orders, the subsidiaries must be closed down. There are measures to prevent the use of the foreign incorporation of subsidiaries as a tactic for removing some commercial operations from direct scrutiny by the Canadian government. For instance, the incorporation of subsidiaries must be approved by the federal Cabinet. All subsidiaries must be disclosed annually to Parliament, or they must be wound up. The potential impact of these measures could be quite significant. During the 1980s as private sector CDIA continues to expand rapidly, government supported foreign operations would actually decline.

SOUTH AFRICA

Canada has historically opposed the racial policies of the Republic of South Africa, and was instrumental in the expulsion of that country from the British Commonwealth during the 1960s. In December, 1977, the Minister for External Affairs, the Hon. Donald Jamieson, announced that the federal government had undertaken a further review of its relations with South Africa. The review had been initiated to ensure that Canadian policies were relatively consistent with those of other countries. It was also aimed at the development of measures which would "demonstrate our disapproval of the present regime and our disapproval of *apartheid*" in the light of contemporary events such as the repression of riots in Soweto township near Johannesburg and the death of black civil rights leader Steve Biko.[37]

As a consequence, the minister announced that all government sponsored commercial-support activities would be phased out, and this included the Export Development Corporation's support for transactions relating to South Africa, such as export credit and loan insurance, as well as foreign investment insurance. Commercial counsellors also would be withdrawn from Johannesburg and Cape Town, although diplomatic relations *per se* would not be severed.

The minister indicated that the government was concerned about the commercial activities which Canadian companies might be carrying out in Namibia as part of their South African operations. Officials from the Ministry of Finance were instructed to determine whether any Canadian firms had received any tax investment concessions from the South African imposed administration in Namibia. Although there should not be any penalization of investments by

> ... Canadian companies that may have been active in that country under legitimate and perfectly acceptable processes. Nevertheless, there is unquestionably an incongruity in a situation that permits an illegal regime, by world definition, to be benefiting with Canadian companies. . .[38]

It was noted that the government would be issuing a code of ethics for those Canadian firms carrying out commercial activities in South Africa, and was considering a code for any investments located in Namibia.

In April, 1978, the Ministry for External Affairs published a code of conduct for Canadian enterprises operating in South Africa, following consultations with several large corporations which would be affected by the policy and with interest groups such as the Task Force on Churches and Corporate Responsibility and the Canadian Labour

Congress.[39] The standard of behaviour has been modelled after, and is basically similar to, a code of conduct for the South African activities of firms based in the EEC which was adopted by the members of the Common Market during September, 1977.

As illustrated in Appendix F, the Canadian code is aimed at limiting any tacit endorsement of the racial policies of the South African government on the part of Canadian firms by setting guidelines for their employment practices. For example, it is recommended that companies should improve the overall work situation of black employees to the fullest extent possible by providing equality of opportunity in terms of work conditions, wages, fringe benefits, training and promotions. Canadian enterprises are urged to integrate workers in their jobs and recreational activities, as well as to limit the use of expatriate white labour. The guidelines stipulate that companies should not impede the ability of employees to organize into, and negotiate via, collective bargaining units, even though non-white trade unions are not officially sanctioned under South African law.

Since March, 1979, all Canadian firms with investments in South Africa have had to publish annual reports which document their adherence to the principles of the code. Relevant criteria include: the number and proportion of blacks employed; the availability of training opportunities for blacks, particularly for advancement to semi-skilled occupations; the manner in which collective bargaining is conducted and the extent of black employee participation in this process; and the level of remuneration for workers. With the exception of the attainment of a wage rate at least 50% above a minimum level necessary to cover living costs, the code does not designate actions which could be considered evidence of compliance; nor did the Canadian government consider it essential to delineate legal penalties for a failure to adhere to the guidelines. However, the Ministry of External Affairs has indicated that an understanding of what would be considered feasible objectives was reached during the consultation with various parties, which took place prior to the publication of the code.[40]

The Canadian guidelines can be distinguished from those adopted by the members of the EEC in several ways. Reflecting differences in social values, the European countries describe adherence to principles of their code as part of the social responsibilities of business, rather than just as desirable objectives. Similarly indicative of varying attitudes towards organized labour, the Canadian guidelines state that companies should ensure that employees are free to organize collective bargaining units, while the European code more forcibly declares that

> Employers should regularly and unequivocally inform their employees that consultations and collective bargaining with organizations are part of company policy. . . . Employers should do everything possible to ensure that black African employees are free to join a trade union. . . .[41]

Canadian authorities historically have been extremely sensitive to the extraterritorial applications of national laws on the part of the parent countries of firms investing inside Canada, particularly the United States. Therefore, it is not surprising that the Canadian code is phrased in a manner which does not explicitly suggest that companies should overtly contravene South African laws while adhering to its principles, even though the code is an extraterritorial application of Canadian moral precepts at the very least. Although acknowledgements are made that the Canadian government objects to some South African legislation and practices, there are no specific citations in the code. In contrast, the European guidelines explicitly condemn several *apartheid* policies, such as the extensive use of migrant labour; and it is recommended that "employers should make it their concern to alleviate as much as possible the effects of the existing system" or "to abolish any practices of segregation."[42]

The Canadian and European governments have taken the position that the forced divestiture of existing commercial activities in South Africa would not provide any tangible benefits to that country's non-white population, and it would prove difficult for companies to liquidate their investments at value. Adherence to the guidelines, however, would provide at least some moderating influence upon the impact of *apartheid* policies. In the Canadian case, the elimination of government commercial-support activities and the increased amount of regulation would represent major disincentives to firms considering the initiation or expansion of operations in South Africa.

The overall impact of the withdrawal of government support for, and the delineation of guidelines on the conduct of, Canadian commercial activities in South Africa, should not be over-estimated. It was noted in Chapter 2 that Canadian direct investment in South Africa amounted to $126 million during 1976, less than 1% of Canadian direct investment abroad. Most of this sum was placed by Canadian firms during the 1960s. As measured by Statistics Canada, the value of these investments has not increased significantly since 1972, and they have decreased as a proportion of total Canadian direct investment abroad.[43] Similarly, South African investment in Canada has been quite limited, and has consisted primarily of a 38.6% interest in Hudson Bay Mining and Smelting by Anglo-American Ltd., and of a 100% interest in Rothman's of Canada Ltd. by Rembrandt Ltd.[44] Canadian trade with South Africa has steadily decreased in absolute dollar volume since 1974. During 1978, Canadian exports to South Africa were worth approximately $112 million, or 0.8% of total exports, while imports from South Africa were valued at $149 million or 0.3% of aggregate imports.[45] Therefore, the amount of trade and investment which will be affected by the policy changes will be relatively small.

Approximately three-quarters of Canadian direct investment

abroad in South Africa has been made by the Canadian subsidiaries of foreign controlled enterprises, such as Ford Canada. Accordingly, efforts by the Canadian government to regulate directly these investments could be impeded or modified by the actions of affiliated firms, and would probably require extensive negotiations with their parent governments.

Finally, although a review was initiated in December, 1977, the Canadian government did not move to terminate the British Preferential Tariff and the Canada-South Africa Trade Agreement of 1932, under which goods imported from South Africa were accorded preferential duty rates. It was not until June, 1979, after a new federal administration was elected, that notice was given that the agreements would be terminated in January, 1980, and that trade would henceforth be subject to the Most-Favoured Nation rates of duty and governed by the General Agreement on Tariffs and Trade. The government did not officially base its decision on moral grounds, but argued that it was taken to ensure a general conformity with other changes resulting from the Tokyo Round of the Multilateral Trade Negotiations. Attention was also drawn to

> . . . the size of the imbalance in preferential trade in South Africa's favour which indicated that there is little economic justification from Canada's point of view for continuing to exchange preferential tariff treatment.[46]

SUMMARY OBSERVATIONS

During the late 1960s and the early 1970s, to a very considerable extent, governments sought to control the nature and behaviour of foreign direct investment through unilateral regulations and legislation. In the Canadian case, this trend was reflected in the creation of FIRA, the introduction of requirements for Canadian citizen participation on corporate boards, and the exclusion of some sectors from foreign investment. However, the viability of this orientation can be limited by the long term ability of many multinational enterprises to shift operations away from those countries where constraints are perceived as unduly restrictive, and by the efforts of parent governments to seek the elimination of host state policies which discriminate on a basis of corporate nationality.

Codes of conduct emerged as an instrument for harmonizing the general rules for the behaviour and treatment of international investment, and this trend should be expected to continue. Existing codes, such as that of the OECD, will probably become more elaborate and issue-specific as less developed countries present demands for a more equitable share in the international economic order. Industrialized nations have indicated a willingness to accept codes of conduct as one means of securing greater legitimacy for multinational enterprises. At the same time, there has been an increased recognition on the part of some less developed countries that the relationship between the nation state and the multinational need not necessarily be antagonistic. When there are clear, consistent rules, which are perceived by all parties as reasonable, cooperation for mutual benefit is possible. This policy orientation could serve as an additional stimulus for the adoption of codes of conduct.

Historically, Canadian governments have been extremely sensitive to the extraterritorial application of laws on firms operating within the country. Nevertheless, one aspect of Canadian codes has been the extraterritorial application of Canadian laws and values. Indeed, as the size and scope of Canadian direct investment abroad continues to expand, it becomes increasingly likely that Canadian governments, like those of other industrialized nations, will view Canadian direct investment abroad as a potential instrument for affecting Canadian foreign policy. Host nations can be expected to object as strenuously to this practice in the future, as Canada has in the past. Indeed, coping with such conflicting pressures may represent the next challenge for Canadian direct investment abroad.

A further challenge for Canadian firms which do business abroad by way of trade and investment is the need to contend with international boycotts which are pursued by other nations. Most notably, certain Arab countries consider their boycott of Israel to be a legimate economic weapon in view of the continuing state of war between Arab countries and Israel. The Canadian government has strongly affirmed its opposition to discrimination and boycotts based on race, religion, or national or ethnic origin.

In its initial statement, on 21 October, 1976, the government condemned boycotts and stated that it would deny its support and facilities, including export financing to firms which complied with unacceptable boycott provisions.[47] The government acted under the provisions of the act which authorises the Department of Industry, Trade and Commerce to assist or withhold assistance from firms in Canada. To date, three reports have been made concerning the administration of Canada's policy on international economic boycotts covering the period 21 October, 1976 to 31 July, 1978.[48] In December, 1978, a bill was introduced which would have made it mandatory for all firms to report requests made for foreign economic boycotts. At present, such reporting is not required and the government only has the power to withhold assistance to firms which comply with boycott requests. This bill died on the order paper prior to the May, 1979 federal election and has yet to be reintroduced.

The final development in this area has been the report by the Hon. R.L. Stanfield on Canada's relations with the Middle East.[49] This report includes some discussion of the need for boycott legislation, and this discussion may be an ingredient in developing future steps which the Canadian government may take. In any event, Canadian business will have to be cognizant of domestic and foreign boycott policies in structuring their future international transactions.

The international growth and geographic expansion currently experienced by an increasing number of Canadian based firms will bring to the surface new issues largely associated with capital exporting activities. This in turn will force the Canadian government to become more actively involved as a parent country participant in national and international deliberations concerning codes of conduct and guidelines.

NOTES

1. T.V. Purcell, "Management and the 'Ethical' Investor", *Harvard Business Review*, Vol. 57, (September-October 1979), pp. 24-25.

2. T. Kennedy, "Investments in Chile to Continue", *Globe and Mail*, 22 April, 1978.

3. H. Schwann, "Origin, Nature, Economic and Political Significance of Codes of Conduct", in European Centre for the Study and Information on Multinational Corporations, *Codes of Conduct for Multinational Companies: Issues and Positions,* (Brussels: ECSIM, 1977), p. 2.

4. USA—BIAC Committee on International Investment and Multinational Enterprise, *A Review of the Declaration on International Investment and Multinational Enterprises,* (New York: USA-BIAC, 1976) p. 13.

5. ICC, *Guidelines for International Investment.*

6. SEC, *Report on Questionable and Illegal Corporate Payments and Payments and Practices,* Submitted to the Committee on Banking, Housing and Urban Affairs, United States Senate, 12 May, 1976, (Washington: Government Printing Office, 1976), pp. 8-9.

7. For a summary of the SEC investigations see N.H. Jacoby, P. Nehemkis, and R. Eells, *Bribery and Extortion in World Business: A Study of Corporate Political Payments Abroad,* (New York: Macmillan, 1978), pp. 45-68.

8. Disclosures to the SEC were originally meant to be confidential in nature. But, to the consternation of some corporations, passage of the Freedom of Information Act resulted in the documents being made accessible to public scrutiny.

9. Jacoby, et al., *op. cit.,* pp. 208-209; L. Silk and D. Vogel, *Ethics and Profits: The Crisis of Confidence in American Business,* (New York: Touchstone, 1976), pp. 225-228; Y. Kugel and G.W. Gruenberg, *International Payoffs: Dilemma for Business,* (Boston: D.C. Heath, 1977), pp. 139-140.

10. R. Hellmann, *Transnational Control of Multinational Corporations,* (New York: Praeger, 1977), p. 68.

11. OECD. *International Investments and Multinationals Enterprises,* (Paris: OECD, 1976), p. 2.

12. Quoted in H. Schwann, "The OECD Guidelines for Multinational Enterprises", *Journal of World Trade Law,* Vol. 12, (1978), pp. 342-343.

13. See Appendix C.

14. See K.P. Sauvant, "Controlling Transnational Enterprises: A Review and Some Further Thoughts", in K.P. Sauvant and H. Haenpflug, eds., *The New International Economic Order: Confrontation or Cooperation between North and South?,* (Boulder: Westview Press, 1977), pp. 356-433.

15. See F. Armstrong, "Political Components and Practical Effects of the Andean Foreign Investment Code", *Stanford Law Review*, Vol. 27, (1975), pp. 1597-1628; C.F. Schill, "The Mexican and Andean Foreign Investment Codes: An Overview and Comparison", *Law and Policy in International Business,* Vol. 6, (1974); Decision No. 24 of the Commission of the Cartagena Agreement, Common Regime of Treatment of Foreign Capital and of Trademarks, Patents, Licenses and Royalties, 31 December, 1970, Registro Official (R.O.) No. 264 (Ecuador), reprinted in *International Legal Materials,* Vol. 126, (1972).

16. Report of the Group of Eminent Persons, *The Impact of Multinational Corporations on Development and on International Relations,* (New York: United Nations, 1973), p. 55.

17. S.J. Rubin, "Harmonization of Rules: A Perspective on the U.N. Commission on Transnational Corporations", *Law and Policy in International Business,* 8(1976), p. 886.

18. See UNCTAD, *Report of the Intergovernmental Group of Experts on an International Code of Conduct on Transfer of Technology on Its Fourth Session.,* (New York: United Nations, 1978), Annexes I and II.

19. See P. Jeffries, "Regulation of Transfer of Technology: An Evaluation of the UNCTAD Code of Conduct", *Harvard International Law Review,* Vol. 18, (1977), p. 331; J.S. Glascock, "Legislating Business Morality: A Look at Efforts by Two International Organizations to Deal with Questionable Behavior by Transnational Corporations", *Vanderbilt Journal of Transnational Law,* Vol. 10, (1977), p. 473; R.C. Wesley, "Problems in Regulating the Multinational Enterprise: An Overview", *International Lawyer,* Vol. 10, (1976), p. 615.

20. D.J. Plaine, "The OECD Guidelines for Multinational Enterprises", *International Lawyer,* Vol. 11, (1977), pp. 343-344; ECSIM, *Values and Limitations of Codes of Conduct as Regulating Instruments for Multinational Corporations,* (Brussels, ECSIM, 1977), p. 59.

21. J. Davidow and L. Chiles, "The United States and the Issue of the Binding or Voluntary Nature of International Codes of Conduct Regarding Restrictive Business Practices", *American Journal of International Law,* Vol. 72, (1978), p. 255.

22. O. Schacter, "The Twilight Existence of Nonbinding International Agreements", *American Journal of International Law,* Vol. 71, (1977), p. 304.

23. "How to Make Business Behave", *The Economist,* (8-14 October, 1977), p. 89.

24. See OECD, *International Investment and Multinationals Enterprises, Review of the 1976 Declaration and Decision, Paris, 1979;* and OECD, *International Investment and Multinational Enterprises, Guidelines for Multinational Enterprises, Paris, Revised Edition, 1979.* The Canadian government's support of this review is contained in a statement by the Hon. Flora MacDonald, 13 June, 1979.

25. Ministry for External Affairs, Public Affairs Communique, "Notes for a statement made by the Secretary of State for External Affairs, the Honourable Allan J. MacEachen, at the OECD Ministerial Meeting in Paris, 21 June, 1976: Investment Issues and Guidelines for Multinational Enterprises."

26. *Ibid.*

27. See OECD, *National Treatment for Foreign-Controlled Enterprises Established in OECD Countries*, (Paris: OECD, 1978), pp. 5-23, and 45-52.

28. For detailed case illustrations of how these criteria are applied refer to Foreign Investment Review Agency, *Annual Report, 1974-1975*, pp. 5-6, 10; *Annual Report, 1975-1976*, pp. 73-86; *Annual Report, 1976-77, pp. 11-13; Annual Report, 1977-1978*, pp. 12-15, 55-59.

29. OECD, *National Treatment for Foreign-Controlled Enterprises*, pp. 10, 13-15.

30. Michael Walker, "Measuring Government Intervention", paper presented at the Canadian Investment Seminar, University of Western Ontario, London, Ontario, 12 July, 1978, p. 22.

31. Privy Council Office, *Crown Corporations: Direction, Control, Accountability — Government of Canada's Proposals*, (Ottawa: Supply and Services), 1977, pp. 13-14.

32. For a detailed analysis of the issues and events see "Second Report of the Standing Committee on Public Accounts", House of Commons, (The Polysar Report), 7 July, 1977.

33. For a detailed analysis of the issues and events see House of Commons, Votes and Proceedings, 27 February 1978 (no. 21), pp. 408-426.

34. House of Commons, *Debates,* 16 December, 1976, p. 2,069.

35. *Ibid.*

36. *Ibid.*, p. 2,070.

37. External Affairs Canada, "Canadian Policy Towards South Africa", *Statements and Speeches*, (N0. 77/23), p. 1.

38. *Ibid.*, p. 2.

39. Ministry of External Affairs, Public Affairs Communique, 28 April, 1978.

40. *Ibid.*

41. "Code of Conduct for Companies with Subsidiaries, Branches or Representation in South Africa", *Bulletin of the European Communities,* Vol. 10, (September, 1977), p. 46.

42. *Ibid.*, p. 47.

43. Statistics Canada, *Canada's International Investment Position, 1968-1970,* pp. 27, 31; *Canada's International Investment Position, 1974*, p. 54.

44. Statistics Canada, *Intercorporate Ownership, 1972,* (Cat. 61-513), (Ottawa, 1974), pp. 339, 415.

45. Statistics Canada, *Imports by Countries: January-December 1978*, (Cat. 65-006), (Ottawa, 1979), pp. 13, 16; *Exports by Countries: January-December 1978,* (Cat. 65-003), (Ottawa, 1979), pp. 11, 14.

46. Ministry of External Affairs, Public Affairs Communique, 15 June, 1979.

47. Statement by the Secretary of State for External Affairs, House of Commons, 21 October, 1976.

48. Department of Industry, Trade and Commerce, *International Economic Boycotts,* First semi-annual report (21 October, 1976 to 31 July,

1977, Second semi-annual report (1 August, 1977 to 31 January, 1978, and Third semi-annual report (1 February, 1978 to 31 July, 1978).

49. Final Report of the Special Representative of the Government of Canada Respecting the Middle East and North Africa, 20 Feb., 1980.

Conditions of Investment Insurance Protection Offered by the Export Development Corporation

TERMS OF INSURANCE

Cover for all investments is limited to a maximum period of 15 years. The minimum period of coverage for equity investment is not fixed, but it is anticipated that most investments in this category will be of a lasting nature. On the other hand, debt investments should normally be of at least three or four years in duration. Short term commercial credit arrangements such as revolving lines of credit or open accounts are normally not eligible for insurance coverage under this programme but may be eligible under EDC's Export Credits Insurance Programme.

COVERAGE UNDER THE PROGRAMME

The maximum amount of coverage available at any one time for each of the three major risks is up to 150% of the dollar amount of the original investment for *equity* securities. The additional amount is to allow protection for retained earnings of up to 50% of the original investment. Insurance for investments in *debt* securities covers the principal amount outstanding plus the amount of accrued interest unpaid in connection with the investment, up to an overall maximum of 150% of the dollar amount of the original principal investment. In the case of the management and technical services agreements, insurance covers the payment receivable for services rendered to an overall maximum of the annual payment receivable times the term of the agreement.

For each of the three risk categories the investor must select a *maximum amount* and a *current amount* of coverage. For example, in the case of equity, the maximum amount is an amount of up to 150% of the original investment and is the upper limit of protection that is available during the life of the contract of insurance and must be declared prior to the execution of the contract. The current amount is the total protection in effect during any one period of 12 months and reflects the anticipated amount to be on risk during a contract year and is declared on the anniversary date of the policy. It must reflect the actual amount on risk at the time. The difference between the maximum amount and the current amount is the *standby amount* which provides for a reserve which the investor can utilize as his investment grows. Additionally, the current amount can change annually at the discretion of the investor on any anniversary date of the contract.

Example: (i)   Amount of total investment is $3.0 million.

(ii) Investor can select coverage of up to $4.5 million (*Maximum Amount*) under one or more of the three major risks.

(iii) If a *Current Amount* of coverage of $1.0 million is selected for a given risk, then

(iv) the balance remaining of $3.5 million is the *Standby Amount.*

Once chosen, the maximum amount can never be increased over the life of the contract whereas the current amount can increase up to the maximum amount in existence on any anniversary date. Both the maximum and current amounts can be reduced under the following circumstances:

(1) if the investor elects to do so on any anniversary date; or

(2) if a claim is paid, both amounts would be reduced automatically for each risk by the amount of the claim.

In the second case, the current amount could be raised again on the anniversary date of the contract only to an amount not exceeding the revised maximum amount for each risk. However, the maximum amount once lowered cannot be raised under the contract of insurance for the same investment.

Coverage under a Policy can have a term of up to 15 years and can be cancelled by the investor, and not by EDC, as long as the conditions of the Policy are maintained. The rate of premium for the coverage of the three risks calculated on the Current Amount is 1% per annum. The investor, however, has a degree of flexibility in his selection of coverage. This allows him to cover only those assets that he actually has at risk and permits him to select Standby Coverage on those amounts not at risk. The investor normally must take all three categories of risks but under special circumstances this may be modified. This choice of coverage usually results in a substantial reduction in the premium costs to the investor. This is reflected in the average premium rate of 7/10 of 1% per annum on total coverage issued to date.

CO-INSURANCE

The insurance investor is normally responsible for 15% of losses on coverages of up to $10 million and 25% of losses on coverages exceeding $10 million. The co-insurance is determined by employing a weighted average of the two percentages and is applied as illustrated below:

(1) For insurance contracts where the maximum amount of cover is any amount up to $10 million the co-insurance factor is a flat 15%. If the investor suffers a $4 million loss on an investment where he has previously elected a current amount in excess of $4 million and his maximum amount is $8 million, then he would be reimbursed $4 million less the 15% co-insurance or $3.4 million.

(2) For insurance contracts where the maximum amount of cover exceeds $10 million the co-insurance factor will be greater than 15%. The factor is determined by adding 85% of the first $10 million (i.e. $8.5) to 75% of the balance exceeding $10 million then dividing this sum by the total maximum amount. This answer is subtracted from 100% to determine the co-insurance factor.

   If the maximum amount is $16 million then 75% of $6 million is $4.5 million which, when added to $8.5 million, equals $13.0 million. Dividing this sum by the total maximum amount of $16 million equals .8125 or 81.25%. Subtracting this percent from 100% gives us the co-insurance factor of 18.75%. Therefore, if the investor suffers a $12 million loss on an investment where he has previously elected a current amount in excess of $12 million and his maximum amount is $16 million then he would be reimbursed $12 million less the 18.75% co-insurance or $9.75 million.

Note The foregoing examples only deal with co-insurance and the application of other parts of the insurance contract may have a bearing on final results. For large or sensitive projects a higher rate of co-insurance may be charged.

COST OF COVERAGE

There are two types of charges levied on the investor for a contract of insurance.

(i) *Handling Fee:*

   This is a *one-shot* fee and will be charged at the rate of 1/10 of 1% of proposed investment with a minimum of $200 and a maximum of $1,000. The purpose of this fee is to cover administrative expenses. It will be levied at the first extension of the waiver letter or when a Letter of Offer is issued, whichever occurs first.

(ii) *Insurance Rates Per Annum:*

	RISK "A" (Inconverti-bility)	RISK "B" (Expropriation)	RISK "C" (War, Revolution and Insurrection)
Insurance Rate on Current Amounts per Risk	0.3%	0.4%	0.3%
Insurance Rate on Standby Amount per Risk	0.125%	0.125%	0.125%

If all risks are fully covered the fee will be a maximum of 1% per annum of the current amount.

COMMENCEMENT OF COVER

Coverage shall take effect the day on which the insurance contract is executed by the Corporation.

CLAIMS

The Canadian investor must give prompt, written notice to EDC of any action, or impending action or any particular situation, which might give rise to a claim under the contract of insurance. The investor may file a claim with EDC upon the happening of certain events and after the passage of normal waiting periods as follows:

    (i) for incovertibility: (these periods may be extended under certain situations).

        (a) 30 days from date of active blockage of funds by a foreign exchange control law, order, decree or regulation;

        (b) 120 days from date of passive blockage of funds by exchange control authorities;

        (c) immediately after the investor has transformed currency (with EDC approval), at a rate of exchange which yields less than the effective free market rate or some such rate agreed upon by the investor and EDC.

    (ii) for expropriation:

        One year from the date the host government commenced the action which unduly restricted the investor from carrying on his business or forced him to give up some or all his rights to his assets.

    (iii) for war, revolution and insurrection:

        Immediately after the event occurs and losses identified.

Note: For war risk only, claims under the insurance contract must exceed either $10,000 or 10% of the current amount insured for the contract year, whichever is smaller. Where the amount of loss exceeds the above, payment will be based on the full amount of loss in accordance with the terms of the insurance contract.

It should be noted that for all risks, the investor's losses are indemnified in the proportion that the coverage carried by him bears to the value of the investment at the time of loss.

Example: If an investor elects to carry $10 million of insurance on an investment of $15 million and he suffers a $9 million loss then he is reimbursed 10/15 or 2/3 of $9 million which equals $6 million less the 15% co-insurance or $5.1 million.

RECOVERIES

Any recovery received by the Corporation after the payment of a claim will be divided between the Corporation and the investor in the same proportion as that which applied to the original loss.

Source: Export Development Corporation, *Foreign Investment Guarantee Programme,* 1 February, 1978, pp. 4-8.

Appendix B

(i) Inco Limited, Form 8-K, (ii) Massey-Ferguson Ltd., Form 8-K

INCO LIMITED

Item 5. Other Materially Important Events

Introduction and Background

This Current Report on Form 8-K reports questionable payments and practices of the Company (which term includes the registrant and its subsidiaries, including ESB Incorporated ("ESB"), a company acquired effective August 1, 1974) during the period 1971 through 1976 which have been revealed as a result of a recently completed investigation and also records the adoption of an expanded and formal policy regarding questionable payments. In the registrant's opinion the matters set forth herein are not material in relation to the operation or financial condition of the Company, whose annual sales for the period have ranged from approximately $800 million to $2 billion. The filing of this Current Report does not constitute an acknowledgement of the materiality of its contents.

The investigation confirmed that, during the more than six years covered, there had been no illegal political contributions, no unlawful payment which was significant in amount, no involvement of any Director or Officer of the registrant in any illegal or improper activity, and, with the few exceptions noted in this report, no improper accounting practices. The Company is concerned, however, with the few deviations from its high standards which the investigation has revealed. Questionable payments revealed in the course of the investigation include principally, in aggregate during the period covered by the investi-ation, *facilitating* payments which did not exceed $240,000, improper payments of $130,000 by certain foreign units of ESB, principally to functionaries of foreign governments, and overbillings as hereinafter described. The Company, therefore, has taken or is taking the corrective steps described below.

On the basis of information derived from its normal auditing procedures, the Company has conducted a broad investigation to determine whether, during the period from the beginning of 1971 to the dates of the interviews (Spring, 1977), any corporate funds had been used to make illegal, improper or questionable payments. The investigation covered all principal locations of the Company and included all principal locations of ESB for the entire period under consideration. Information as to AB Tudor, a Swedish company acquired by ESB on January 31, 1977, is not included herein.

Pursuant to the advice of the registrant's outside counsel, Sullivan & Cromwell, and the registrant's independent accountants, Price Waterhouse & Co., the registrant's Comptroller and its Chief Legal Officer established procedures for carrying out the investigation. During the course of the investigation, interviews were conducted with approximately 250 officers, employees and former employees, representing about 60 operating and staff units with responsibilities for substantially all of the Company's business.

On April 19, 1977, an interim report was made to the registrant's Audit Committee, all of whom are non-management Directors, and the registrant's Board of Directors. Further reports were made to the Audit Committee and to the Board on July 6 and July 21, 1977.

At their respective July 6, 1977 meetings, the Audit Committee recommended, and the Board of Directors adopted, a statement setting forth the Company's Guidelines on Business Conduct which is attached hereto as Exhibit (a). The guidelines prohibit entirely, or, in a few instances, emphasize the stringent nature of the limitations to be observed with respect to, each practice referred to in this Current Report, without regard to whether such practice is material.

Questionable Payments Disclosed by the Investigation

A number of units* have made facilitating payments to government personnel in various foreign countries to expedite the performance of duties which the recipient was obligated to perform in any event, such as the issuance of various permits and documents. The total amount of such payments in the survey period did not exceed $240,000; no individual payment was significant in amount and the great bulk of these payments did not exceed $100. This amount includes payments believed to have been made to foreign customs personnel by customs brokers who were retained in certain countries abroad for the purpose of assisting in

---

*As used herein, a *unit* is a subsidiary or operating division of the Company's metals business or of ESB.

customs clearance. In most instances, the customs brokers were reimbursed in certain countries abroad for the purpose of assisting in customs
clearance. In most instances, the customs brokers were reimbursed
upon submission of invoices, some of which may have reflected disbursements to government officials as well as non-government broker-
age disbursements. Most of the sums believed to have been paid to
government officials in the form of facilitating payments were recorded
on the books of the unit making the payments, in some cases without
proper identification, except that in the case of the ESB organization, a
few payments were made from certain off-book accounts referred to
below. The above total amount does not include cash payments in one
foreign country where there are no published schedules of fees for
such governmental services as issuing motor vehicle registrations and
drivers' licenses, work permits, visas and immigration document. In that
country, in accordance with local practice, fees are paid to the functionary
performing the service and receipts are frequently not available.
Facilitating payments were made only in those countries where such
payments were customary, even though some of them may have been
unlawful. The company intends to eliminate such payments wherever
possible, but taking into account whether there is any practical necessity
for such payments if units are to continue doing business in certain
foreign countries. Accordingly the Guidelines on Business Conduct set
forth the conditions limiting their continuance.

Several foreign units of ESB paid amounts totalling $130,000 to
functionaries of foreign governments and to others in apparent violation
of local law or for other improper purposes, such as obtaining reductions in duty and tax assessments, commercial information, and a business permit. Almost half the payments were made in connection with a
series of government contracts in one foreign country. Certain of these
payments were made from off-book accounts referred to below; the rest
were charged to various expenses and in many cases were not properly
indentified. Under the Guidelines on Business Conduct payments of this
sort are expressly forbidden.

Three foreign units of ESB maintained off-book cash accounts, some
of which were used in making certain of the payments referred to above.
These funds were accumulated in a number of ways. During the period
in question, the highest total amount of funds contained in these
accounts at any time did not exceed $140,000. These accounts have now
been liquidated. The largest of these accounts, which was accumulated
by having one foreign unit overbilled by a supplier, was used to pay the
expenses of that unit requiring hard currency which was not available in
the country of its operation. An unrecorded receivable resulting from
unintentional overpayment of expenses is not included above as an off-
book account; no improper payments were made from this source. The

uncollected balance of this receivable has now been recorded on the books of the Company. Under the Guidelines on Business Conduct there are to be no transactions which are not properly recorded on the books of the Company.

A number of ESB foreign units have billed certain of their distributors at prices in excess of the agreed gross sales prices. The amounts received by such units in excess of the gross sales prices were disbursed by the units as directed by the distributors; in most cases the units were instructed to deposit the funds in bank accounts in the names of the distributors or of third persons outside the countries in which the distributors operated. Although the Company believes that these practices do not involve any violations of law by ESB, they may have simplified violations of local requirements by the distributors involved. The total amount invoiced in excess of gross sales prices during the period under consideration was $1,370,000. Under the Guidelines on Business Conduct, false or improper invoicing practices are prohibited.

In connection with certain foreign operations, several ESB units have understated the value of goods or otherwise provided incorrect information on invoices reflecting shipments to or between foreign countries, and in some instances, foreign customs duties were underpaid or foreign import restrictions were not complied with.

At the request of customers and distributors, units have remitted regular commissions and service fees payable to the customer or distributor to designated third persons or bank accounts in third countries. In some cases the commissions were not shown on the invoices. Such payments will continue to be made only under the following conditions: (i) the amount payable does not arise from artificial additions to normal selling prices, (ii) payment is authorized in writing by the company or person earning the commission or fee, (iii) payment is made to the same entity to which it is owed or to an affiliate with common ownership, and (iv) payment will not cause the Company to violate applicable law.

Level of Approval

None of the unlawful payments was known to the registrant's officers or Directors.

United States Taxes

None of the payments was claimed as a deduction on United States income tax returns. In a few instances some of the payments were inadequately identified and may have resulted in overstatement of foreign tax credits and consequent underpayment of United States income taxes. To the extent that further investigation reveals that amounts were improperly treated for United States income tax purposes, corrective measures will be taken to pay any additional taxes due.

Exhibit (a)
INCO LIMITED
GUIDELINES ON BUSINESS CONDUCT

Introduction

At its July 6, 1977 meeting, the Board of Directors of Inco Limited adopted the following policy guidelines on business conduct. These rules apply to Inco Limited and its subsidiaries (the Company) and set out standards of propriety in the areas covered.

The basic principles herein are to guide our dealings with all our constituencies, particularly our customers and suppliers, and the communities and governments in the countries where we have operations or otherwise do business.

It is the responsibility of each employee to assure compliance with this policy. Management employees receiving copies of these guidelines are to ensure that the Company's policy is communicated to all those employees reporting to them who could be faced with a situation covered by it. In addition, management employees have a continuing responsibility to review conformance with the Company's policy.

Our employees are assured that continued strict observance of these standards, even at the risk of adverse business consequences, will be supported by the senior management of Inco Limited. Deviation from them, on the other hand, will be grounds for appropriate disciplinary or other action.

General Policy of Adherence to Ethical Standards

Employees are to act in accordance with the highest standards of fairness, integrity and equity.

General Policy of Adherence to Law

Employees are to act in accordance with the laws of the jurisdictions in which our business is conducted. It is recognized that employees in some countries may be subjected to local pressures to engage in unlawful conduct, but the interests of the Company will be served best in the long run if such pressures are resisted.

While illegal conduct can take many forms, two types are worthy of special mention.

(a) Political Contributions

In jurisdictions where corporate political contributions are prohibited by law, no Company assets are to be used in any manner, directly or indirectly, for such purposes. In countries where corporate political contributions are lawful, none is to be made except where specifically authorized by the Chairman, or, in his absence, the President of Inco Limited.

(b) Unlawful Payments

No unlawful payment is to be made to secure or maintain business, to influence any decision relating to the Company's business or affect the enactment or enforcement of any laws or regulations or to obtain other favors. No employee of the Company is to offer or make an illegal gift or any other form of illegal payment — for example, a bribe or kickback — or enter into (or authorize on the Company's behalf) any illegal agreement or arrangement — such as by way of fee, rebate or consultancy agreement — for such purpose. The purpose of this policy is to prohibit such payments, gifts or arrangements to or with any public or private individual including officials, employees and representatives of political bodies, governments and their branches and agencies, private corporations and organizations doing business or otherwise having dealings with the Company.

Facilitating Payments

In a few countries minor government officials may demand small facilitating payments for performing routine administrative functions they are in any event required to perform. In these locations such conduct even though unlawful or of doubtful legality may not only be customary but it may be part of the locally understood and accepted compensation arrangements for minor posts. These situations should be distinguished from situations where the Company makes payments not in violation of local law to a government agency for government services, such as security services, which are not intended to be prohibited by these guidelines.

As a matter of policy the Company is opposed to the making of facilitating payments and will take steps wherever possible to minimize or eliminate such payments. In no event, however, are they to be made unless they are clearly necessary to the Company's essential business needs. No facilitating payment is to be made unless it has been authorized by the senior officer in the country concerned, it is made outside such countries as Canada and the United States and it is not made for corrupt motives, that is, with the intent to induce the recipient to misuse his official position, and only if the amounts are reasonable in relation to the services performed, receipts are obtained wherever practicable and the country manager submits at least quarterly to the Comptroller of Inco Limited a listing of these types of payments detailed as to payee, amount and purpose.

Proper Accounting

The Company's books of account are to reflect properly all transactions in accordance with the highest standards of integrity. There are to be no cash funds, bank accounts, investments or other assets which are either not recorded or are inadequately recorded on the books of the Company. The Company shall not maintain an unidentified account at any bank.

The use of *false invoices* or other misleading documentation, and the making of fictitious entries for any purpose whether regarding sales, purchases or any other Company activity are prohibited.

No payments are to be made directly or indirectly, in cash other than: (i) regular, approved cash payrolls, (ii) normal disbursements from petty cash accounts which are supported by signed receipts or other appropriate documentation, and (iii) disbursements for necessary business purposes in those countries where payments by cash rather than by check are customary and therefore required in the regular conduct of business.

Since payments into unidentified bank accounts may give rise to suspicion that the Company is participating in an improper transaction, no payments of any nature are to be made into unidentified bank accounts or other accounts which are not clearly or completely identified as to their ownership.

Third Country Payments

Customers and distributors have sometimes requested that their regular commissions or service fees be remitted to third persons or bank accounts in third countries. Such payments will continue to be made only under the following conditions: (i) the amount payable does not arise from artificial additions to normal selling prices, (ii) payment is authorized in writing by the company or person earning the commission or fee; (iii) payment is made to the same entity to which it is owed or to an affiliate with common ownership, and (iv) payment will not cause the Company to violate applicable law.

Implementation

Supplementary guidelines may from time to time be issued to add or to clarify these guidelines should the need to do so develop.

In order to ensure continued compliance with these policy guidelines, a certificate in substantially the following form shall be signed annually by April 1 of each year by all persons (and their successors in office) who have received this letter, and submitted to the Comptroller of Inco Limited:

Within the past 30 days I have read the Guidelines on Business Conduct and any supplementary guidelines to it of Inco Limited and its subsidiaries and I have satisfied myself that to the best of my knowledge no breach of the Guidelines, as supplemented, has occurred since (date) except those instances, if any, reported by me for remedial action.

In signing this certificate I am relying where necessary on certificates in the same form signed by certain employees who report to me.

. . . .
(Signature)

. . . .
(Date)   (Title)

MASSEY-FERGUSON LIMITED

To the Shareholders:

Report to United States Securities and Exchange Commission

On December 23, 1977, the Company filed an 8-K report with the Securities and Exchange Commission. An amended report was filed in January, 1978. The report dealt with the subject of *questionable payments.*

The Company's 8-K filing wiht SEC was voluntary and follows the practice of U.S. corporations, including our major competitors. Massey-Ferguson is one of the few Canadian companies registered with the SEC. There is no provision or requirement for similar filings with securities commissions in Canada.

In the opinion of the Company, the information in the 8-K report was not material relative to the Company's operations nor was any action disclosed which is illegal in Canada or the United States or in any of the countries in which Massey-Ferguson has operating facilities.

Details of the 8-K filing, including a statement of Company Policy on Standards of Business Conduct, are as follows:

In the spring of 1977, under the guidance of senior management, and later the Audit Committee of the Board of Directors of Massey-Ferguson Limited ("Company"), an investigation was commenced with respect to possible practices and payments by the Company and its subsidiaries in categories which might be considered to be questionable.

The Company is a holding company located in Toronto, Canada; its operations are located in subsidiaries throughout the world. Wherever the word *year* is used herein, it refers to the Company's fiscal year ending October 31. When the word *foreign* is used it refers to countries other than Canada and the United States.

The investigation, which covered the five-year period ended

October 31, 1977, was conducted by the Company's Assistant Comptroller-Audit with the assistance of the Company's Legal Services Director-Corporate. The investigation involved extensive interviews with and questioning of officers and employees and examination of records at many locations throughout the world. At the conclusion of the investigation, the findings were reported by the Assistant Comptroller-Audit to the Audit Committee and subsequently by the Audit Committee to the Board of Directors. The findings are summarized as follows:

1. The investigation disclosed no instances of slush funds or illegal political contributions in any country nor of legal political contributions in an amount which might be expected to result in any special governmental consideration for the interest of the Company or a subsidiary. In addition, except to the extent specifically noted below no cases were found where receipts or payments had been improperly recorded in the books of the Company or any subsidiary.

The Directors and corporate officers of the Company ("Senior Management") were not, prior to the investigation, aware of the events set forth herein except as to those matters where such knowledge is specifically described.

2. No instances were found of payments to government officials to obtain special consideration for the interests of the Company or any of its subsidiaries, with the following two exceptions:

(i) In each of the years 1973 and 1974, a foreign government official who was instrumental in having his government place orders with one of the Company's subsidiaries (amounting to approximately $789,000 in 1973 and $1,511,000 in 1974), was paid approximately $12,000 in cash. These payments were made out of general funds of the subsidiary without receipts being obtained and were recorded on the subsidiary's books as miscellaneous expenses and, at the direction of the official, were paid outside his own country. The payments were legal in the country in which the Company's subsidiary operated and in the country in which the payments were made. The Company does not know whether such payments were illegal under the laws of the country in which the foreign official was resident or the reasons for directing that payments be made outside such country, but believes that the reasons may have been to evade or violate legal requirements and/or detection by local authority in such country. One member of Senior Management was aware of this transaction.

(ii) Cases may have existed where nominal amounts may have been paid to minor foreign government employees to facilitate the obtaining of services to which the Company was entitled. Since any such nominal amounts would have been included as a sundry item in the employee's expense report, it has not been possible to quantify the total amounts.

3. Courtesy gifts of modest value have been made to, or exchanged with, some government officials, bankers and others with whom the Company's subsidiaries conduct business. In 1977, these gifts aggregated approximately $46,000 in value and covered approximately 1,500 gifts ($31 per average gift). The three largest gifts were $724 (silver plate), $390 (clock) and $200 (music box). These gifts were recorded as such in the subsidiaries' books. In the opinion of the Company the giving of such gifts is a normal expression of courtesy or regard and does not constitute a questionable practice. The Company will continue to give such gifts in appropriate situations.

4. Three instances were found in which sales commissions, so recorded on the books, were paid by certain of the Company's foreign subsidiaries in connection with sales resulting from competitive tenders in circumstances that raised questions as to whether the commission or some portion thereof may have been remitted ultimately to one or more government officials or to other parties who might influence the tender awards. These commissions were paid, respectively, to a non-governmental publicly owned company, to a non-governmental distributor of the Company, and to a non-governmental individual who was a former distributor of the Company; the recipients represented that they would be able to be of assistance in obtaining the sales for the Company's subsidiaries. The commissions involved in these transactions aggregated $2.4 million and the related net sales aggregated $12.6 million, and the commissions making up such aggregate were higher than commissions normally paid by the Company. The Company does not have evidence in any of these instances that any commission or portion thereof was in fact remitted to government officials, or other parties, or was used to make any illegal payments. At least three members of Senior Management were aware that one or more of such sales commissions were being paid.

5. Prior to 1974, a foreign corporation ("manufacturer") in which the Company has a minority interest, under normal contractual provisions in a marketing agreement, paid a commission to one of the Company's foreign subsidiaries for such subsidiary's work as agent for the sale of the manufacturer's products throughout the world. Commencing in 1974, the commission was reduced. The manufacturer, however, continued to pay commissions at the original rate. The difference amounted to $195,000 in 1974, and of this $88,000 was subsequently paid to the shareholders of the manufacturer. The remainder was returned to the manufacturer. In 1975, the difference amounted to $197,000 of which $119,000 was paid through the subsidiary to the manufacturer's shareholders and $78,000 to a bank account of the manufacturer outside the country where the manufacturer was located. On the Company's initiative, this practice ended with the 1975 year. The above-described transactions may have aided in avoiding, or involved the manufacturer in violation of, certain foreign taxes and foreign exchange

controls. The receipt of such funds by the foreign subsidiary was recorded as miscellaneous income and the payments by the subsidiary was charged to the same account.

6. In making what the Company considers to have been proper and appropriate allocations of revenues and expenses among certain of the Company's subsidiaries, the Company overbilled or underbilled other subsidiaries of the Company in order to transfer funds, the transferability of which might otherwise have been restricted or been subject to delays under foreign controls such as price controls, local content regulations, foreign exchange regulations, tax and banking regulations. The following situations were found (with one or more members of Senior Management having been aware of the situation set out in paragraphs (i), (iii) and (v) below:

(i) In 1975 one subsidiary billed and collected from another subsidiary for certain air freight shipments. Under Company rules, the shipping subsidiary should have absorbed the excess cost of air freight over sea freight which amounted to approximately $250,000. Instead of refunding such excess cost, the funds were retained by the shipping subsidiary and used by it to pay expenses of the receiving subsidiary for which the receiving subsidiary was experiencing difficulty in obtaining foreign exchange clearances.

(ii) In 1977 one subsidiary undertook to reimburse certain of its distributors for airfare incurred by them in attending a tractor demonstration. The fares involved aggregated approximately $12,000. Upon learning that it would take many months to obtain the necessary foreign exchange approvals to pay the fares, a second subsidiary paid them out of funds owed to the first subsidiary.

(iii) Prior to 1977, volume rebates of approximately $600,000 annually were received on certain components by one subsidiary which retained such rebates and so recorded them on its books. The rebates related to world-wide purchases of such components by several subsidiaries. Commencing in 1977, the rebate has been apportioned among the subsidiaries on the basis of actual purchases by them.

(iv) One subsidiary owed its distributors approximately $400,000 for commissions, warranty claims, etc., which has been accruing since 1971 but which had not been paid due to the subsidiary's inability to obtain necessary foreign exchange permits. In 1977, a second subsidiary paid the amounts owing (the largest single payment being $82,400), in return for which the first subsidiary paid expenses incurred by the second subsidiary in the country of the first subsidiary.

(v) During the five year period ended October 31, 1977, one subsidiary underbilled another subsidiary by $2,145,000 for components sold to it for local assembly. This was done in order to improve the domestically produced percentage of the end product. The underbilled amount was recovered by withholding amounts otherwise due to the purchasing subsidiary. This practice has now been stopped.

(vi) During 1972 through 1975, one subsidiary failed to record commissions aggregating approximately $296,000 owed to it by two other subsidiaries. The two other subsidiaries paid an aggregate amount equal to the unrecorded commissions to the Company and other subsidiaries to pay expenses owed to them by the first subsidiary.

(vii) In 1974 a corporation in which the Company owns a minority interest sold goods to a subsidiary but was unable to collect $280,000 of the purchase price because of exchange control regulations in the subsidiary's country. In 1975 this corporation sold goods to a second subsidiary and thereafter was unable to pay $84,000 to such subsidiary on a defective parts claim because of such corporation's own exchange control problems. By means of special discounts, the second subsidiary paid such corporation $196,000 (representing the net of the amount such corporation was owed by the first subsidiary and the amount such corporation owed to the second subsidiary). To compensate the second subsidiary for making such payment on its behalf, the first subsidiary commenced to underbill the second subsidiary for products shipped. After $100,000 had been underbilled, this practice was discontinued.

The recording of the foregoing transactions in the books of the Company and its subsidiaries in the manner indicated had no material effect on the financial statements of the subsidiaries concerned or on the Company's consolidated financial statements.

7. The Company's sales into countries in which it does not have manufacturing operations are, with minor exceptions, made to distributors located in such countries. At the request of some distributors, subsidiaries supplying such distributors have raised the sales price of goods sold to them and arranged for the settlement of the amount of the overpayment according to the distributors' directions. In some cases the overbilled amount is remitted to the distributors in the country where he operates, but in the majority of cases payment is made in another country to or upon the order of the distributor. The possibility exists that these arrangements may serve a purpose of a distributor which is illegal in the country where the distributor operates. Certain invoices and related documents delivered in connection with such sales contain certifications which are required by the law of the distributor's country and which, in some cases, were inaccurate because they did not reveal the agreement to remit the overbilled amount.

The investigation disclosed that over the five year period ended

October 31, 1977, sales involving overbillings took place in connection with the following percentage of the Company's consolidated net sales:
1973-3.8%   1974-3.5%   1975-3.6%   1976-3.3%   1977-4.4%
In each of these years the total amount of overbillings and their relationship to Company sales were as follows:

Total Overbilled	Relationship to Affected Sales	Relationship to Total Sales
1973-$4.4 million	7.7%	29/100 of 1%
1974-$5.3 million	8.6%	30/100 of 1%
1975-$7.2 million	7.9%	29/100 of 1%
1976-$6.1 million	6.6%	22/100 of 1%
1977-$7.2 million	6.0%	26/100 of 1%

In all cases the amounts overbilled were netted against sales revenue in the Company's consolidated statements of income. Consequently, no distortion of the figures for consolidated net sales took place.

Members of Senior Management, other than outside Directors, were generally aware of the overbilling practices.

In addition to the foregoing, it has come to the Company's attention that a foreign corporation in which the Company has a minority interest made a small political contribution in a foreign country which may have been illegal. Neither the Company nor any of its subsidiaries or employees had any involvement in or knowledge of this matter.

In the opinion of the Company, none of the matters discussed in this Report will have any material effect on present or future operations of the Company and its subsidiaries or on their income tax or other liabilities. Furthermore, the Company does not believe that any of such matters will result in criminal charges being brought against the Company or its subsidiaries in the countries involved.

Following is a statement of the Company Policy on Standards of Business Conduct adopted by the Executive Committee of the Board of Directors of the Company on December 16, 1977 pursuant to the recommendation of the Audit Committee of the Board of Directors. It is the Company's intention to eliminate all overbilling practices as promptly as possible and in any event no later than the end of the Company's current fiscal year. As set forth in paragraph 7 of such Company Policy, "payments in nominal amounts to minor foreign, (i.e., non-Canadian and non-U.S.), government employees to facilitate the obtaining of services to which the Company is entitled may be continued to the extent such payments are in accordance with custom and established practice in the country involved, and are judged to be necessary in order to avoid obstruction or unreasonable delay." In the opinion of the Company, all other questionable payments and practices of the Company and any of its subsidiaries have been eliminated.

COMPANY POLICY ON STANDARDS OF BUSINESS CONDUCT

1. The business of the Company and its subsidiaries is to be conducted in accordance with the letter and spirit of the laws of the various countries in which business is carried on and in accordance with the highest ethical standards of business conduct.

2. The use of Company or subsidiary funds, facilities or assets for any unlawful purpose is prohibited.

3. All assets, liabilities and transactions of the Company and its subsidiaries shall be recorded in the regular books of account, promptly, fully and accurately. In particular:

(i) No undisclosed or unrecorded fund or asset shall be maintained outside the normal system of accountability for any purpose.

(ii) No transaction shall be recorded or carried out in a manner such that the substance of the transaction is obscured or recorded improperly.

4. All commissions or other fees paid or accrued for agents or other representatives shall be in accordance with sound business practice, for legitimate commercial reasons, and reasonably related in value to the services performed. When there is reason to suspect that all or part of any commission may be used for improper payments, the responsible Company or subsidiary officer must satisfy himself that such will not be the case.

5. Political contributions may be made only where they are legal and in accordance with local custom. All contributions must be restricted to amounts small enough to negate any impression that special consideration for the Company is sought.

6. All transactions between the Company and any of its subsidiaries or between any of such subsidiaries will meet all applicable legal requirements.

7. Payments in nominal amounts to minor foreign, (i.e. non-Canadian and non-U.S.), government employees to facilitate the obtaining of services to which the Company is entitled may be made to the extent such payments are in accordance with custom and established practice in the country involved, and are judged to be necessary in order to avoid obstruction or unreasonable delay.

8. All overbilling practices will be eliminated as promptly as possible and in any event no later than the end of the Company's current fiscal year.

9. Adherence to these policies is to be monitored by the Company's internal and external auditors.

Appendix C

The OECD Guidelines

Annex to the Declaration of 21st June 1976 by Governments of OECD Member Countries on International Investment and Multinational Enterprises.

GUIDELINES FOR MULTINATIONAL ENTERPRISES

Multinational enterprises now play an important role in the economies of Member countries and in international economic relations, which is of increasing interest to governments. Through international direct investment, such enterprises can bring substantial benefits to home and host countries by contributing to the efficient utilisation of capital, technology and human resources between countries and can thus fulfil an important role in the promotion of economic and social welfare. But the advances made by multinational enterprises in organising their operations beyond the national framework may lead to abuse of concentrations of economic power and to conflicts with national policy objectives. In addition, the complexity of these multinational enterprises and the difficulty of clearly perceiving their diverse structures, operations and policies sometimes give rise to concern.

The common aim of the Member countries is to encourage the positive contributions which multinational enterprises can make to economic and social progress and to minimise and resolve the difficulties to which their various operations may give rise. In view of the transnational structure of such enterprises, this aim will be furthered by co-operation among the OECD countries where the headquarters of most of the multinational enterprises are established and which are the location of a substantial part of their operations. The guidelines set out hereafter are designed to assist in the achievement of this common aim and to contribute to improving the foreign investment climate.

Since the operations of multinational enterprises extend throughout the world, including countries that are not Members of the Organisation, international co-operation in this field should extend to all States. Member countries will give their full support to efforts undertaken in co-operation with non-member countries, and in particular with developing countries, with a view to improving the welfare and living standards of all people both by encouraging the positive contributions which multinational enterprises can make and by minimising and resolving the problems which may arise in connection with their activities.

Within the Organisation, the programme of co-operation to attain these ends will be a continuing, pragmatic and balanced one. It comes within the general aims of the Convention of the Organisation for Economic Co-operation and Development (OECD) and makes full use of the various specialised bodies of the Organisation, whose terms of reference already cover many aspects of the role of multinational enterprises, notably in matters of international trade and payments, competition, taxation, manpower, industrial development, science and technology. In these bodies, work is being carried out on the identification of issues, the improvement of relevant qualitative and statistical information and the elaboration of proposals for action designed to strengthen inter-government co-operation. In some of these areas procedures already exist through which issues related to the operations of multinational enterprises can be taken up. This work could result in the conclusion of further and complementary agreements and arrangements between governments.

The initial phase of the co-operation programme is composed of a Declaration and three Decisions promulgated simultaneously as they are complementary and inter-connected, in respect of guidelines for multinational enterprises, national treatment for foreign-controlled enterprises and international investment incentives and disincentives.

The guidelines set out below are recommendations jointly addressed by Member countries to multinational enterprises operating in their territories. These guidelines, which take into account the problems which can arise because of the international structure of these enterprises, lay down standards for the activities of these enterprises in the different Member countries. Observance of the guidelines is voluntary and not legally enforceable. However, they should help to ensure that the operations of these enterprises are in harmony with national policies of the countries where they operate and to strengthen the basis of mutual confidence between enterprises and States.

Every State has the right to prescribe the conditions under which multinational enterprises operate within its national jurisdiction, subject to international law and to the international agreements to which it has subscribed. The entities of a multinational enterprise located in various countries are subject to the laws of these countries.

A precise legal definition of multinational enterprises is not required for the purposes of the guidelines. These usually comprise companies or other entities whose ownership is private, state or mixed, established in different countries and so linked that one or more of them may be able to exercise a significant influence over the activities of others and, in particular, to share knowledge and resources with the others. The degree of autonomy of each entity in relation to the others varies widely from one multinational enterprise to another, depending on the nature of the links between such entities and the fields of activity concerned. For these reasons, the guidelines are addressed to the various entities within the multinational enterprise (parent companies and/or local entities) according to the actual distribution of responsibilities among them on the understanding that they will co-operate and provide assistance to one another as necessary to facilitate observance of the guidelines. The word *enterprise* as used in these guidelines refers to these various entities in accordance with their responsibilities.

The guidelines are not aimed at introducing differences of treatment between multinational and domestic enterprises; wherever relevant they reflect good practice for all. Accordingly, multinational and domestic enterprises are subject to the same expectations in respect of their conduct wherever the guidelines are relevant to both.

The use of appropriate international dispute settlement mechanisms, including arbitration, should be encouraged as a means of facilitating the resolution of problems arising between enterprises and Member countries.

Member countries have agreed to establish appropriate review and consultation procedures concerning issues arising in respect of the guidelines. When multinational enterprises are made subject to conflicting requirements by Member countries, the governments concerned will co-operate in good faith with a view to resolving such problems either within the Committee on International Investment and Multinational Enterprises established by the OECD Council on 21st January 1975 or through other mutually acceptable arrangements.

Having regard to the foregoing considerations, the Member countries set forth the following guidelines for multinational enterprises with the understanding that Member countries will fulfil their responsibilities to treat enterprises equitably and in accordance with international law and international agreements, as well as contractual obligations to which they have subscribed:

General Policies

Enterprises should
   (1) take fully into account established general policy objectives of the Member countries in which they operate;
   (2) in particular, give due consideration to those countries' aims and priorities with regard to economic and social progress, including industrial and regional development, the protection of the environ-

ment, the creation of employment opportunities, the promotion of innovation and the transfer of technology;

(3) while observing their legal obligations concerning information, supply their entities with supplementary information the latter may need in order to meet requests by the authorities of the countries in which those entities are located for information relevant to the activities of those entities, taking into account legitimate requirements of business confidentiality;

(4) favour close co-operation with the local community and business interests;

(5) allow their component entities freedom to develop their activities and to exploit their competitive advantage in domestic and foreign markets, consistent with the need for specialisation and sound commercial practice;

(6) when filling responsible posts in each country of operation, take due account of individual qualifications without discrimination as to nationality, subject to particular national requirements in this respect;

(7) not render — and they should not be solicited or expected to render — any bribe or other improper benefit, direct or indirect, to any public servant or holder of public office;

(8) unless legally permissible, not make contributions to candidates for public office or to political parties or other political organisations;

(9) abstain from any improper involvement in local political activities.

Disclosure of Information

Enterprises should, having due regard to their nature and relative size in the economic context of their operations and to requirements of business confidentiality and to cost, publish in a form suited to improve public understanding a sufficient body of factual information on the structure, activities and policies of the enterprises as a whole, as a supplement, in so far as necessary for this purpose, to information to be disclosed under the national law of the individual countries in which they operate. To this end, they should publish within reasonable time limits, on a regular basis, but at least annually, financial statements and other pertinent information relating to the enterprise as a whole, comprising in particular:

(1) the structure of the enterprise, showing the name and location of the parent company, its main affiliates, its percentage ownership, direct and indirect, in these affiliates, including shareholdings between them;

(2) the geographic areas* where operations are carried out and the principal activities carried on therein by the parent company and the main affiliates;

(3) the operating results and sales by geographic area and the sales in the major lines of business for the enterprise as a whole;

(4) significant new capital investment by geographic area and, as far as practicable, by major lines of business for the enterprise as a whole;

(5) a statement of the sources and uses of funds by the enterprise as a whole;

(6) the average number of employees in each geographic area;

(7) research and development expenditure for the enterprise as a whole;

(8) the policies followed in respect of intra-group pricing;

(9) the accounting policies, including those on consolidation, observed in compiling the published information.

Competition

Enterprises should, while conforming to official competition rules and established policies of the countries in which they operate,

(1) refrain from actions which would adversely affect competition in the relevant market by abusing a dominant position of market power, by means of, for example,

    a) anti-competitive acquisitions,

    b) predatory behaviour toward competitors,

    c) unreasonable refusal to deal,

    d) anti-competitive abuse of industrial property rights,

    e) discriminatory (i.e. unreasonably differentiated) pricing and using such pricing transactions between affiliated enterprises as a means of affecting adversely competition outside these enterprises;

(2) allow purchasers, distributors and licensees freedom to resell, export, purchase and develop their operations consistent with law, trade conditions, the need for specialisation and sound commercial practice;

---

*For the purposes of the guidelines on disclosure of information the term *geographic area* means groups of countries or individual countries as each enterprise determines is appropriate in its particular circumstances. While no single method of grouping is appropriate for all enterprises or for all purposes, the factors to be considered by an enterprise would include the significance of operations carried out in individual countries or areas as well as the effects on its competitiveness, geographic proximity, economic affinity, similarities in business environments and the nature, scale and degree of interrelationship of the enterprises' operations in the various countries.

(3) refrain from participating in or otherwise purposely strengthening the restrictive effects of international or domestic cartels or restrictive agreements which adversely affect or eliminate competition and which are not generally or specifically accepted under applicable national or international legislation;

(4) be ready to consult and co-operate, including the provision of information, with competent authorities of countries whose interests are directly affected in regard to competition issues or investigations. Provision of information should be in accordance with safeguards normally applicable in this field.

Financing

Enterprises should, in managing the financial and commercial operations of their activities, and especially their liquid foreign assets and liabilities, take into consideration the established objectives of the countries in which they operate regarding balance of payments and credit policies.

Taxation

Enterprises should:

(1) upon request of the taxation authorities of the countries in which they operate, provide, in accordance with the safeguards and relevant procedures of the national laws of these countries, the information necessary to determine correctly the taxes to be assessed in connection with their operations, including relevant information concerning their operations in other countries;

(2) refrain from making use of the particular facilities available to them, such as transfer pricing which does not conform to an arm's length standard, for modifying in ways contrary to national laws the tax base on which members of the group are assessed.

Employment and Industrial Relations

Enterprises should, within the framework of law, regulations and prevailing labour relations and employment practices, in each of the countries in which they operate,

(1) respect the right of their employees to be represented in trade unions and other bona fide organisations of employees, and engage in constructive negotiations, either individually or through employers' associations, with such employee organisations with a view to reaching agreements on employment conditions, which should include provisions for dealing with disputes arising over the interpretation of such agreements, and for ensuring mutually respected rights and responsibilities;

(2) a) provide such facilities to representatives of the employees as

   may be necessary to assist in the development of effective collective agreements,

   b) provide to representatives of employees information which is needed for meaningful negotiations on conditions of employment;

(3) provide to representatives of employees where this accords with local law and practice, information which enables them to obtain a true and fair view of the performance of the entity or, where appropriate, the enterprise as a whole;

(4) observe standards of employment and industrial relations not less favourable than those observed by comparable employers in the host country;

(5) in their operations, to the greatest extent practicable, utilise, train and prepare for upgrading members of the local labour force in co-operation with representatives of their employees and, where appropriate, the relevant governmental authorities;

(6) in considering changes in their operations which would have major effects upon the livelihood of their employees, in particular in the case of the closure of an entity involving collective lay-offs or dismissals, provide reasonable notice of such changes to representatives of their employees, and where appropriate to the relevant governmental authorities, and co-operate with the employee representatives and appropriate governmental authorities so as to mitigate to the maximum extent practicable adverse effects;

(7) implement their employment policies including hiring, discharge, pay, promotion and training without discrimination unless selectivity in respect of employee characteristics is in furtherance of established governmental policies which specifically promote greater quality of employment opportunity;

(8) in the context of bona fide negotiations* with representatives of employees on conditions of employment, or while employees are exercising a right to organise, not threaten to utilize a capacity to transfer the whole or part of an operating unit from the country concerned in order to influence unfairly those negotiations or to hinder the exercise of a right to organise;

(9) enable authorised representatives of their employees to conduct negotiations on collective bargaining or labour management relations issues with representatives of management who are authorised to take decisions on the matters under negotiations.

---

*Bona fide negotiations may include labour disputes as part of the process of negotiation. Whether or not labour disputes are so included will be determined by the law and prevailing employment practices of particular countries.

Science and Technology

Enterprises should:
  (1) endeavour to ensure that their activities fit satisfactorily into the scientific and technological policies and plans of the countries in which they operate, and contribute to the development of national scientific and technological capacities, including as far as appropriate the establishment and improvement in host countries of their capacity to innovate;
  (2) to the fullest extent practicable, adopt in the course of their business activities practices which permit the rapid diffusion of technologies with due regard to the protection of industrial and intellectual property rights;
  (3) when granting licenses for the use of industrial property rights or when otherwise transferring technology do so on reasonable terms and conditions.

Canadian Guidelines

Guiding Principles of Good Corporate Behaviour in Canada (1966)*

Seeking to encourage and facilitate full and appropriate participation of Canadian subsidiaries of foreign companies in Canada's growth and development, the Minister wrote to the chief executive officers of some 3,500 such firms. His letter set forth 12 guiding principles of good corporate behaviour. It emphasized the need for foreign subsidiaries in Canada to strive for maximum realization of their potential and for full participation in and identification with Canadian interests.

The letter also sought the co-operation of the larger foreign owned subsidiaries in providing periodic information, on a confidential basis, relative to certain aspects of their operations and financing.

With company replies naturally varied in relation to the different principles, responses from senior management indicated a large general measure of conformity and a willingness on the part of most companies progressively to pursue policies in line with the Minister's objectives. Many companies also stated that they had found the statement helpful in suggesting the direction corporate thinking might take for the mutual benefit of company operations and Canada's trade, economic and social needs.

The objectives set forth by the Minister as a guide toward achieving and maintaining good corporate citizenship were as follows:

(1) Pursuit of sound growth and full realization of the company's productive potential, thereby sharing the national objective of full and effective use of the nation's resources.

(2) Realization of maximum competitiveness through the most effective use of the company's own resources; progressively achieving appropriate specialization of product development within the international group of companies.

(3) Maximum development of export opportunities.

(4) Extension of processing of natural resource products to the economically practicable maximum.

(5) Pricing policies aimed at assuring a fair and reasonable return to

---

*Seventy-Fifth Annual Report, Department of Trade and Commerce, 1966, pp. 18-20.

the company and to Canada for all goods and services sold abroad, including sales to the parent company and other affiliates.

(6) To search out and develop economic sources of supply of parts and materials within Canada.

(7) To develop, as an integral part of the Canadian operation wherever practicable, the capability for technological research and design necessary to pursue product development programs and thus to take full advantage of market opportunities domestically and abroad.

(8) Retention of sufficient earnings to give appropriate financial support to expansion of the Canadian operation while ensuring fair return to shareholders.

(9) To work toward a Canadian outlook within management, through training programs, promotion of qualified Canadian personnel and inclusion of a major proportion of Canadian citizens on its Board of Directors.

(10) To achieve a financial structure which provides opportunity for equity participation by Canada.

(11) Periodically to publish information on financial position and operations.

(12) To give appropriate attention and support to recognized national objectives and established government programs designed to further Canada's economic development; to encourage and support Canadian institutions directed toward intellectual, social and cultural advancement.

Principles of International Business Conduct (1975)*

Foreign controlled businesses in Canada are expected to operate in ways that will bring significant benefit to Canada. To this end they should pursue policies that will foster their independence in decision making, their innovative and other entrepreneurial capabilities, their efficiency, and their identification with Canada and the aspirations of the Canadian people.

Within these general objectives, the following principles of good corporate behavior are recommended by the Canadian government. Foreign controlled firms in Canada should:

(1) Pursue a high degree of autonomy in the exercise of decision making and risk taking functions, including innovative activity and the marketing of any resulting new products.

(2) Develop as an integral part of the Canadian operation an autonomous capability for technological innovation, including research, development, engineering, industrial design and prepro-

---

*Foreign Investment Review Agency. A Businessman's Guide to the Foreign Investment Review Act, (Ottawa, 1976).

duction activities; and for production, marketing, purchasing and accounting.

(3) Retain in Canada a sufficient share of earnings to give strong financial support to the growth and entrepreneurial potential of the Canadian operation, having in mind a fair return to shareholders on capital invested.

(4) Strive for a full international mandate for innovation and market development, when it will enable the Canadian company to improve its efficiency by specialization of productive operations.

(5) Aggressively pursue and develop market opportunities throughout international markets as well as in Canada.

(6) Extend the processing in Canada of natural resource products to the maximum extent feasible on an economic basis.

(7) Search out and develop economic sources of supply in Canada for domestically produced goods and for professional and other services.

(8) Foster a Canadian outlook within management, as well as enlarged career opportunities within Canada, by promoting Canadians to senior and middle management positions, by assisting this process with an effective management training program, and by including a majority of Canadians on boards of directors of all Canadian companies, in accordance with the spirit of federal legislative initiatives.

(9) Create a financial structure that provides opportunity for substantial equity participation in the Canadian enterprise by the Canadian public.

(10) Pursue a pricing policy designed to assure a fair and reasonable return to the company and to Canada for all goods and services sold abroad, including sales to parent companies and other affiliates. In respect of purchases from parent companies and affiliates abroad, pursue a pricing policy designed to assure that the terms are at least as favourable as those offered by other suppliers.

(11) Regularly publish information on the operations and financial position of the firm.

(12) Give appropriate support to recognized national objectives and established government programs, while resisting any direct or indirect pressure from foreign governments or associated companies to act in a contrary manner.

(13) Participate in Canadian social and cultural life and support those institutions that are concerned with the intellectual, social, and cultural advancement of the Canadian community.

(14) Endeavour to ensure that access to foreign resources, including technology and know-how, is not associated with terms and conditions that restrain the firm from observing these principles.

Appendix E

Government Policy and Guidelines Concerning the Commercial Practices of Crown Corporations

Statment by the Honourable Robert Andras, President of the Treasury Board on Government Policy and Guidelines Concerning the Commercial Practices of Crown Corporations, December 16, 1976.

Mr. Speaker,

We are all aware that an increasingly competitive atmosphere in international trade has led in the post-war period to trading arrangements and business practices which are not always in keeping with the legal and ethical standards of Canada and other countries.

In recent years, both the private and public sectors in several countries have been working toward an improved code of conduct governing the promotion of international trade. Accordingly, I wish to state today the policy of the Government of Canada on the conduct which is expected of Canadian Crown corporations and, more particularly, on the commercial practices of these corporations.

To put the issue in perspective, we must recognize as a fact of life the constant tension between the twin goals of promoting foreign trade and, at the same time, maintaining standards of conduct, on the part of Canadians and their agents, which can stand up to the closest public scrutiny.

This is not a new problem, nor is it restricted, in its broader dimensions, to the field of international trade. Each of us is familiar, in our lives, with the way in which our ethical judgements define acceptable and unacceptable methods of pursuing personal goals. In the process of making such judgements, both governments and individuals discern that some actions are clearly unacceptable because they are obviously in conflict either with the law of the land or with fundamental principles of behaviour which individuals or societies have adopted as their own.

Other actions are just as clearly discerned to be perfectly consistent with both the law and ethical principles.

But there is a middle area, a grey area, where difficulties can and do arise. In this middle area fall those practices about which people who consider themselves to be of equal integrity can make differing judgements, practices whose ethical quality can be perceived differently in different societies, and even within the same society at different stages of its development.

The existence of this grey area demands that those responsible for the conduct of others provide guidance. It demands as well that such guidance be re-examined periodically to keep it relevant to changing circumstances, maturing values, and newly developed practices.

For an exporting country like Canada, whose economic health is largely determined by its success in selling its goods and services abroad, the way in which that trade is carried out is of major importance to the country as a whole.

That is why the Government of Canada is heavily involved, and properly so, in promoting our products and helping private Canadian companies sell their goods and services to foreign customers. In the case of Crown corporations involved in the export trade, the level of government involvement in sales promotion and trade is even more pronounced.

To appreciate how vital these efforts are to the economy of the country, one need only note that 25% of all jobs in Canada are related to our export trade, as is some 23% of the income of Canadians, and about 56% of the goods produced in this country.

Because international trade is a matter of life or death for Canada, the government and the people of this country are naturally concerned about any development which might jeopardize our trading activity or damage our external and trade relations.

In the recent past, we have had reason for concern. First, there have been over the past few years revelations about unacceptable business practices, including bribery, which involved corporations and governments in other parts of the world. These revelations have shocked the international community, disrupted governments, and cast a disturbing shadow over the international trading environment.

In response, the governments of Canada and other countries have taken remedial action. The international community, within the United Nations and the Organization for Economic Co-operation and Development, is making a determined effort to establish a code of conduct suited to the problems which have come to our attention. Canada has supported and will continue to support such efforts.

The second reason for concern is that, here at home, questions have recently been raised about the business and accounting practices of certain Crown corporations involved in the export trade, such as Polysar and Atomic Energy of Canada Limited.

In response, the government has referred these questions to the Public Accounts Committee of the House. The government is giving the Committee its full co-operation, in the confidence that we will receive sound and helpful advice at the conclusion of its deliberations.

As a further response, the government has formalized the guidelines governing the commercial practices of Canadian Crown corporations.

With a view to providing both protection and guidance, I will now state these guidelines:

(1) In the process of doing business, officials of Federal Crown corporations shall not, directly or indirectly:

(i) take any action in Canada that is not in accordance with the laws of Canada, or take any action outside Canada that violates the laws of the place where the transaction occurs, or that if taken in Canada would be in violation of the Criminal Code of Canada;

(ii) render or accept any bribe or other improper benefit;

(iii) apply improper influence.

(2) In retaining sales and procurement agents, Crown corporations shall adhere to the following:

(i) *Selection*

Crown corporations must adopt an established selection process to ensure that the agents' qualifications for the work are clearly established and evaluated.

(ii) *Contracting*

a. Agency agreements shall be formally written and shall include specific undertakings by the agents to act in accordance with the laws of the place where the transaction occurs.

b. Remuneration under the Agreements shall be based on justifiable and sound business practice.

c. Payments shall be strictly in accordance with the formal written agreement.

(iii) *Approval*

a. The Board of Directors or other governing body of each corporation shall establish a procedure for approval of agency agreements.

b. The Board of Directors or other governing body may approve any exception from the administrative aspects of this policy where it is satisfied such exception is warranted.

(iv) *Disclosure*

a. Corporations will disclose in their annual reports the names of their agents, as well as the aggregate of all remuneration paid to such agents.

b. Any approved administrative exception from the policy and the reasons therefor shall be disclosed in the annual report of the corporation.

Such is the Government's policy and such are the guidelines governing the commercial practices of Crown corporations.

Code of Conduct Concerning the Employment Practices of Canadian Companies Operating in South Africa

In South Africa there are policies, legislation and practices based on the principle of racial discrimination which are repugnant to Canadians, and which the Canadian Government has condemned as contrary to internationally-accepted standards of human rights. Many Canadians are concerned about the extent to which companies identified with Canada are involved in South Africa in an economic system based on racial discrimination.

The Canadian Government has noted that a number of Canadian companies have already shown leadership in establishing programs to improve the working conditions of the non-White employees of their affiliates in South Africa. It strongly hopes that every Canadian company active in that country will promote employment practices which are based on the principle of equal treatment for all its employees, and which are consistent with basic human rights and the general economic welfare of all people in South Africa. While these objectives are applicable to all employees, they have particular relevance to the employment conditions of Black African workers. The Government believes that, by promoting the achievement of these objectives, Canadian companies will be able to make an important contribution towards improving the working conditions generally of Black and other non-White workers in South Africa.

The Government commends to Canadian companies the Declaration adopted unanimously in 1973 by the Executive Committee of the International Organization of Employers. Among its other provisions this declaration "appeals to the Republic of South Africa to fulfill its obligations in respect of human rights and to repeal its discriminatory legislation with the aim of giving equal rights and protection of those rights to all workers and in particular by guaranteeing:

— equality of opportunity in respect of admission to employment and training;
— equality in conditions of work and respect for the principle of equal pay for equal work; and
— freedom of association and the right to organize and collective bargaining."

The Declaration also appeals to "to all employers in South Africa to take urgent measures to promote the conditions necessary for acceptance of the well established standards in the field of human rights approved by the International Labour Organization." The Government believes Canadian companies should implement the above-mentioned principles of the Declaration of the International Organization of Employers, which were reaffirmed by the I.O.E. in June, 1977.

Accordingly, it is the view of the Canadian Government that:

(1) *General Working Conditions*

In general companies should improve the overall work situation of Black employees to the fullest extent possible, and ensure that employment practices applicable to any group of workers are equally applicable to all workers.

(2) *Collective Bargaining*

Companies should ensure that their employees are free to organize collective bargaining units that can effectively represent them, and undertake to engage in collective bargaining with such units in accordance with internationally-accepted principles. As companies are aware, under South African law Black trade unions are not registered trade unions officially empowered to negotiate industrial council agreements, but such organizations are not illegal. Companies should extend customary basic rights to such bargaining units, that is, to organize for the purpose of negotiation, to solicit support among employees, to disseminate trade union information material, and to engage in other traditional trade union activities on company premises.

(3) *Wages*

Companies should ameliorate the effects of the job reservation and job classification system by implementing the principle of equal pay for equal work — that is, the staffing of and remuneration for a position should be based on the qualifications of an individual and not on his racial origin. They should also strive to provide remuneration sufficient to assist their Black employees in particular to achieve a standard of living significantly above the minimun level required to meet their basic needs. The Canadian Government endorses the widely accepted guideline that the minimum wage should initially exceed this minimum level by at least 50%.

(4) *Fringe Benefits*

> Companies should provide to Black workers improved fringe benefits such as contributory medical and pension plans, disability insurance schemes, sick leave benefits and annual vacations. Companies should ensure that any benefits available to one group of employees is available to all employees. The Canadian Government encourages companies to assist in providing for their staff adequate medical and health facilities for them and their families, transportation to and from their place of work, adequate housing, education for their children and other social services such as legal assistance and unemployment insurance.

(5) *Training and Promotion*

> Companies should provide training programs and job opportunities to facilitate the movement of Blacks into semi-skilled and skilled positions and introduce Blacks to supervisory positions on an accelerated basis, rather than recruiting expatriate personnel.

(6) *Race Relations*

> Companies should, to the fullest extent possible, integrate their working, dining, recreational, educational and training facilities. Companies should seek the advice and assistance of such South African organizations as the Institute of Race Relations and the National Development and Management Foundation which have done extensive studies of the problem of worker productivity and efficiency and which can provide invaluable advice on ways to find solutions which benefit both workers and companies.

The Canadian Government intends to follow developments closely. Canadian companies operating in South Africa should make annual public reports in sufficient detail to permit assessment of their progress in realizing the objectives of the Code of Conduct.

Index